UNLOCK
THE POWER OF YOUR
PERCEPTION

UNLOCK THE POWER OF YOUR PERCEPTION

Claim Your Natural Strengths

Reframe Your Weaknesses

Reshape Your Most Important Relationships

Lynda-Ross Vega
Gary M. Jordan, PhD

Paperback – ISBN 978-0-9816288-8-2
Hardcover – ISBN 978-0-9816288-7-5

Our Gift to You

In this book, you will discover the key to unlocking your natural strengths is understanding your Perceptual Style.

Are you curious about
what your Perceptual Style might be?

We've created an introductory sample assessment
just for YOU!

Just use the link below
to gain instant access to our free assessment:
https://www.yourtalentadvantage.com/PSI

To our parents:

Commander Robert Ross and Mercedes L. McFarland

Drs. J. Russell and Lois F. Jordan

It's not what you look at that matters,
it's what you see.

—Henry David Thoreau

Table of Contents

Our Story

"Gee, I think I'll develop some self-awareness today. That might come in handy one day," said no one, ever.

The truth is, none of us seek out self-discovery unless we think there is something wrong—with us or with the people around us.

There's always an underlying problem:

- "Why don't they see it my way?"
- "What's wrong with them?"
- "What's wrong with me?"
- "Why can't I be like her?"
- "Why isn't my value recognized?"
- "Why are they making it so hard?"
- "Why do we always argue?"

The specific questions are endless, but they have a common theme—feeling frustrated that something we want or expect is eluding us.

These feelings of frustration that something is missing are universal. They happen to all of us at one time or another.

Scott is 37 years old. He has a job he likes (for the most part) in a tech company he's been with for several years. He's enjoyed recognition for his work and has received several promotions. He has a family he loves and friends he enjoys. But even with his success to date, he feels something is missing.

Scott is struggling with what he assumes is work-life balance—not enough time in the day, forgoing things he wants to do for things he feels he has to do, both at work and at home. He's tired. He's not as satisfied as he thought he'd be. He's not as happy as he thought he'd be. So, he's feeling frustrated and wonders what's wrong with him.

Maybe you recognize Scott, or maybe you've been in a similar spot yourself—feeling you are missing something or need to fix something, that you aren't fitting in or measuring up, or that you aren't as happy or fulfilled or successful as you want to be.

It's pretty common in those situations to conclude there must be something wrong with you.

Truth is, there probably isn't anything wrong with you except that you aren't living life using your natural strengths.

Instead, it's likely you are focused on filling weaknesses you think you have rather than using your natural strengths as your foundation.

In the process of pursuing relationships, developing a career, and living life in general, it's so easy to lose awareness of who you are in pursuit of who you think you need to be.

Being human is hard work. Our basic DNA is designed for us to live in community with other people. We all want to be understood, valued, and loved; to belong, to matter.

The reality is, as humans we pursue our need for community for our entire lives.

The frustration that comes with the experience of not fitting in, not measuring up starts in early childhood for everyone. We, the authors of this book, are not exceptions.

For this book's co-author Gary, it was frustration about feeling like an outsider in his own family growing up. Gary's parents were both accomplished medical doctors—his mother was the first female OB/GYN to open a private practice in Dallas. Theirs was a loving home, but one that strongly discouraged Gary's natural curiosity, energy, and desire for experiential learning in life in favor of a studious, mistake-adverse, and accomplishment-oriented environment. It dampened his spirit and his appreciation for his own strengths.

The frustration that this book's co-author Lynda-Ross experienced growing up began with the death of her father (and namesake Robert Ross) when she was 11. Her sudden realization that life wasn't guaranteed and the grief that enveloped her family for years accelerated her drive to resolve problems and desire to make everyone happy. As a result, she pushed her awareness of her own strengths into the background while focusing on everyone else.

Gary earned his PhD in clinical psychology. He found in psychology an avenue to explore human behavior and the concepts of individual strengths that had always intrigued him. He was at the forefront of the positive psychology movement as he explored ways to incorporate strength development in therapy.

Lynda-Ross was intrigued with sociology and earned an associate degree in police administration. Quickly realizing she was more interested in crime prevention than law enforcement, she shifted her focus to working in the corporate world, eventually specializing in change leadership. Along the way, she found something missing in the business world—a reliable way to identify the most qualified people for specific tasks, so they could do more of what they do best, thus enhancing the productivity of the whole.

We, Gary and Lynda-Ross, met in 1984. Lynda-Ross was an executive in a technology company, looking for tools to help her lead people through the complexities of long, demanding projects. She reached out to the corporate head of human resources for advice. He put her in touch with Gary, who was shifting his focus from private practice in clinical psychology to executive coaching.

We bonded over the concepts of style theories. Psychological style theories are designed to help us understand the reasons and motivations behind human emotions and behaviors. Gary's PhD dissertation was on that subject, and he incorporated style theory concepts into his therapy and coaching approach.

Lynda-Ross was a style theory enthusiast, exploring them to help her find the answers on how to match the right people to the right tasks. She knew from experience that placing people in roles where they flourished directly impacted timelines, work quality, and employee satisfaction. The challenge was finding the right tools to help people uncover their strengths.

Over the next several years, we collaborated to build on the work Gary had begun using in his doctoral thesis and practical experience as a therapist and to incorporate the organizational and management experience of Lynda-Ross.

Our goal was to create a tool that would help people identify and value their own strengths and avoid the frustrations of feeling less than or not fitting in.

We know that building your life on your strengths provides a sense of well-being and satisfaction. It also opens the door to recognizing and valuing other people's strengths and provides the insights to spot and defuse disconnects with the people you care about.

Our work is solidly based on behavioral psychology, style theory concepts, clinical and practical research, and observation. We've tested our ideas by designing and delivering style-based coaching and training in corporate settings on topics such as leadership, change, teamwork, conflict, and mastering specific job functions. The core of our work was, and continues to be, our commitment to helping individuals identify their natural strengths and build on those strengths in all aspects of their lives.

By 1994 we had completed our research and theory development groundwork, including creating assessments to demonstrably measure Perceptual Style and developed strengths. In this way Perceptual Style Theory™ was born, grounded in behavioral psychology and real life.

The work didn't stop there. Over the years, we've refined the theory, automated and refined the assessments, and conducted multiple research studies to test reliability and validity.

We are constantly expanding the library of reference materials for each Perceptual Style, delivering coaching and certification programs, and just having fun living our own lives and running our business based on our own natural strengths.

This Book

The purpose of this book is to help you unlock the power of your natural strengths and begin the process of intentionally using them in your life. We've organized the information into three sections:

Section 1 is about the science of behavioral theories and Perceptual Style Theory in particular. It introduces you to the history of how and why behavioral style theories came into use and provides some comparison information about the different approaches to style theories. Then it explores the key concepts of Perceptual Style Theory in detail.

Section 2 introduces you to the six Perceptual Styles. There are highlights of each style and a discussion about the theoretical relationships between styles. You'll see yourself and people in your life reflected in the styles. We encourage you to take the free assessment offered at the front of this book so that you have an idea of your possible Perceptual Style—it makes reading about the styles more fun!

Section 3 is all about the practical application of Perceptual Style in your life. You will learn the steps to identify and claim your own natural strengths. You will also learn how to recognize the strengths in other people and how to spot and mitigate disconnects. The awareness you'll gain will transform the way you understand human differences.

We recommend reading the sections in order as the easiest way to build your knowledge.

You will also find the sections to be excellent reference tools as you build your own strength repertoire, understand differences between you and other people, practice seeing the best in others, and mitigate disconnects with the people who matter to you.

Let's get started!

SECTION 1

The Concepts of Perceptual Style Theory

Megan knows from experience that there are people she connects with easily and people she just doesn't click with. There are people who interest her and others who bore her to tears. There are family members she adores, but she wonders if they feel the same about her.

She has coworkers who all share the same passion for the work they do, but who approach it so differently from her. Is there a right way and a wrong way? Does the process matter if the end results are the same?

At times Megan doubts herself. Is her inability to understand and get along with everyone because there is something wrong with her? How can she fix whatever that is? Is there anything to fix?

Megan is not alone with these questions. Throughout time people have searched for ways to understand each other. It is not easy. But there are tools that can help, and style theories are some of the best.

An Introduction to Style Theories

If you are curious about the science behind Perceptual Style, then this section is for you. First, we will explore how style theories came to be used, and then we will dive into the details of Perceptual Style Theory.

In science, a theory presents a concept or idea that is testable.[1] A theory is not merely a guess; it's a fact-based framework for describing, explaining, and predicting behaviors.[2]

Psychological style theories are designed to help us understand the reasons and motivations behind human emotions and behaviors.

Style theories group commonalities—such as habits, behaviors, and priorities—into "styles." In essence, style theories provide us with easy reference categories that create a shorthand way to help us quickly identify and understand similarities and differences between people.

Psychological theories must have four components:

- Describe behavior.
- Make predictions about future behaviors.
- Have evidence to support the conclusion.
- Be testable.

The first style theory is attributed to Hippocrates, who identified "the four humors" (or temperaments).[3] Hippocrates' work was eventually modified by Plato and further developed by Galen—all before 190 AD! You can also find versions of the four temperaments in some of the style theories of today.

The four temperaments have been given many names along the way:

- Hippocrates (370 BCE) called them blood, black bile, yellow bile, and phlegm (all such appealing labels from the father of medicine).
- Plato (340 BCE) called them artistic, sensible, intuitive, and reasoning (labels for the thinking man.)
- Aristotle (325 BCE) called them iconic, pistic, noetic, and dianoetic (very philosophic).
- Galen (190 AD) called them sanguine, melancholic, choleric, and phlegmatic (another medical perspective).
- Paracelsus (1550 AD) called them salamanders, gnomes, nymphs, and sylphs (pioneer of chemicals and minerals in medicine ... need we say more?).
- Kretschmer (1920) called them manic, depressive, oversensitive, and insensitive (psychology creeps in).
- Keirsey (1978) called them artisan, guardian, idealist, rational (the modern revision).

Other style theories use binary opposite pairs to measure an individual's placement on the continuum between the two extremes. For example, feeling versus thinking is a commonly used binary opposite pair. The continuum measurement determines how much a person prefers each and then reflects where that person falls between the two. Do they feel more than think, or perhaps think more than feel, or maybe do both about equally? These continuum-based style theories describe style as the combination of an individual's placement on multiple (usually three to five) continuums.

Theories that use combinations and continuums allow styles to gently slide from one side of the binary pair to the next. As a result, people believe that their psychological style is based on their situation and that it's changeable over time, which leaves them without an explanation as to why they experience irreconcilable differences with others or why they feel like they have to change to become more functional.

While the concept that one's style changes from situation to situation is comforting—it is ultimately a "cop-out" or "fudge factor." It allows us to avoid facing the concept of limitations—the concept that there are things that we will never do well. Some are because we don't have any interest in them, and many we would like to master, but they draw on strengths that aren't natural for us. No matter how hard we put our mind, effort, and determination into them, mastery eludes us.

Limitations are real, but they aren't something to be afraid of or to deny. Sure, they can be frustrating at times (and we can show you how to deal with that), but more often than not, they serve as a guide to help you focus more on what you do best instead of chasing skills that aren't satisfying.

At the opposite end of the spectrum from limitation is potential. We believe that each person has a multitude of inherent skill potentials associated with their Perceptual Style. It's doubtful anyone could tap into the totality of their potential in one lifetime!

We will explore the concept of limitations and its impact on Perceptual Style Theory in greater detail in Section 3. What is essential to understand at this point is that people do not "slide" from one Perceptual Style to another and that each Perceptual Style describes a unique and fixed perceptual experience.

In the last 80 years, modern style theories have become popular as tools to help explain behavioral, psychological, and emotional differences between people and have emerged as effective tools for personal and organizational development. You've probably been exposed to one or two of them at school or work.

In addition to stylistic differences based on a coherent theory, several tools are also based on empirical observation (relying on experience or experiment). These tools seek to describe differences without providing any underlying theoretical explanation about why the differences exist or where they come from. The self-help section of your local library and bookstores are filled with these.

Theory-based or empirically based, each theory/tool takes a distinctive approach to explain differences in human behavior.

With all this focus on explaining differences between people, it is easy to forget how much we all share. Here's the fascinating thing—as humans, we have a lot more in common than we have differences. In fact, we take our similarities for granted. We all want to belong, be valued, feel in control of our lives, be loved, and feel the power of accomplishment.

We all travel the same basic road of life. We all experience happiness, sadness, illness, tragedy, joy, frustration, love, loss, and death. There are no shortcuts, no avoidance options ... just longer and shorter journeys with varying amounts of each experience.

So, why do people focus on differences?

To understand differences, let's look at similarities first. Most people don't really notice them because they simply take the similarities for granted. Since we don't notice them, we miss how similar all people are. Similarities are assumed, expected. From physical attributes, such as the number of arms and legs, to basic needs, such as food, shelter, clothing, and water, to abstract drives, such as success, accomplishment, status, belonging, and happiness. These are all so "obvious" that we do not even question them.

But differences stand out like a sore thumb: these people don't look like us. These people have different values.

These people eat different food. These people measure success differently.

Differences demand our attention; they challenge our assumptions and threaten our core needs and values. They challenge our beliefs that we have it all figured out. That the way we see the world is the right way. So, we often obsess over them.

Sigmund Freud, Austrian neurologist and the founder of psychoanalysis, coined a term that describes this over-focus on differences—"narcissism of the slight difference"—as a belief that the small things that are different are more important than commonalities. It is the differences between us that get the most attention. We attack others who we perceive as different because we can't both be right, can we? We focus on the differences as a way to make us feel better about ourselves at the expense of others.

But differences and the belief that those who are different from us are "wrong" pushes people apart and drives conflict, communication disconnects, and the experience of being judged as less than.

We watch this play out all the time in politics on the world stage. But it happens every day in family and work situations too. For example, here's a story a friend shared recently with Lynda-Ross. One of Dedra's adult daughters approached her with the idea of a family vacation. Dedra and her husband Mike thought it sounded like a great idea. With three adult children, two with children of their own and all living in different parts of the state, it had been a couple of years since everyone had been together.

With her parents on board, their daughter Lynn reached out to her siblings, Mark and Jennifer, who responded enthusiastically. A family video call was scheduled.

They were perhaps five minutes into the call when the disconnects started to happen. Each person voiced their enthusiasm for a shared vacation, but the reality was, each of them was hoping for something different in the experience.

Dedra wanted to spend time with the grandkids and relive her feelings of family togetherness from years gone by. Mike wanted to strengthen connections with each of his children. He always looked forward to one-on-one time with each of them.

Lynn, the mother of three (ages 6, 8, and 10), wanted to relax and let her hair down. Mark, with two teenage sons, wanted to incorporate lots of outdoor activities. Jennifer, just out of grad school and single, worried that their grandparents and cousins might feel left out. And if anyone had asked, most likely the grandkids would have all said they just wanted to have fun.

In that first call, the family couldn't even agree on a destination. Instead, they decided to schedule another call in a couple of weeks and see if any ideas popped up.

When Dedra shared the story with Lynda-Ross, Dedra's family had just completed call number five, and they just about had all the details worked out. Dedra expressed her relief that it looked like the vacation would be a reality and her surprise that the planning had taken as long as it had.

Even when there is a bond of family love, meeting everyone's expectations can be hard work. The shared desire to be together can quickly be lost if everyone insists that the trip fits only their expectations. Without compromise, the idea of a family vacation can lose its luster, take on the essence of more work than it's worth, and the event will never take place.

That's a common result with disconnects. They can feel like too much work, and it's just easier to dismiss the other person as wrong and walk away.

The question is—why should differences always lead to issues? The answer is—they shouldn't. Differences are what add the spice to life, fueling teamwork, community, and so much more. If we were all exactly alike, the world would be incredibly dull, and most likely, we would have died off as a species.

The world is a complex place that demands we work together, cooperate, respect alternative viewpoints, and accept the challenges they bring. By opening up to what others bring that is different, we can accomplish more than we could each working alone on a project, problem, or crisis.

Understanding differences allows us to appreciate unique strengths, our own and other people's.

When you understand your own strengths and build on that foundation, you gain a new perspective about how you fit in the world, shine a light on your self-worth, and increase your confidence in your ability to handle whatever comes your way.

As you stand in your strengths, you can choreograph your life to follow the path you choose.

Equally important is what comes from understanding and accepting the unique strengths that others bring to the mix. Not all situations require all viewpoints, but many, if not most, can benefit from more than one. Each adds its own value, and the result is a synergistic solution in which the sum is greater than its parts.

Why a New Style Theory?

So far, we have talked generally about psychological theories and style theories and the value they bring. But right now, you may be asking yourself, "Given that there are so many style theories available in the world today, why create a new one? After all, the other ones each provide insights into human behavior." You may be familiar with one or more of the style theories currently available and found them either useful or irrelevant to your life. In either case, why one more?

In our experience, while all style theories will give you some level of information about yourself, they don't all measure the same thing or come to the same conclusions. For example:

- Some start with observation and are based on empirical data while others start with a question based on theory.
- Some are based in psychology and others in biology, behavior, motivation, or spirituality.
- Some seek to explain differences between people, and others are focused only on describing the individual.
- Some are about personality traits, and others are about observable behavior.

That's a lot of differences, and that's just the beginning. The insights gained from each of the other theories we have surveyed are interesting but incomplete. Most have no theoretical foundation, so stop short of helping you understand why things are the way they are, and very few offer concrete ways in which you can use the information they provide to change your life. In other words, they don't answer two essential questions: "Why?" and "What next?"

To answer these two questions is the reason we created Perceptual Style Theory (PST). PST stands out from all the rest because of its unique approach—combining perception with developmental experience—to explain WHY you have the natural strengths you do and answer, "WHAT'S NEXT?" by showing you how to use those strengths more effectively in all aspects of your life.

That's what Perceptual Style Theory is all about.

Key Points

- Style theories group commonalities—such as habits, behaviors, and priorities—into "styles." Style theories provide easy reference categories that allow you to quickly identify and understand similarities and differences between people.
- Psychological theories must have four components. They must describe behavior, make predictions about future behaviors, have evidence to support the conclusions, and be testable.
- In the last 80 years, modern style theories have become popular as tools to help explain behavioral, psychological, and emotional differences between people and have emerged as effective tools for personal and organizational development.
- As humans, we have a lot more in common than we have differences. In fact, we take our similarities for granted.
- It's the differences between us that get the most attention.
- Theory-based or empirically based, each theory/tool takes a distinctive approach to explain differences in human behavior.
- Perceptual Style Theory was created to answer the questions "Why?" and "What next?"

Perceptual Style Theory

Perceptual Style Theory is a contribution to the field of type and style theories, based on the hypothesis that the different ways individuals perceive the world form the basis for their natural potential, strengths, and the way they interact with others.

The real key is understanding perception. Perception is the process of interpreting the different sensations we receive to make meaning of the world around us. It's how we turn the data gathered through our senses into meaningful information about the world. Perception is at the core of who you are.

Have you ever noticed that one of the most basic plots in any crime story is the different viewpoints of the witnesses? It's not just a creative ploy. It's reality.

While we all like to believe that we see the world around us objectively, social psychology calls this "naïve realism"—believing what we see is right and that people who disagree with us must be uninformed, irrational, or biased.[4]

The concept of objective reality is that reality exists independent of our minds. Once we observe, once we process the input from our senses in our mind, it's subjective reality. Differences in perception occur because none of us has direct access to objective reality. It's not because we don't want to; it's just an impossibility. In trying to determine what is true, we can't fully get outside ourselves.

Perceptual Style Theory (PST) explains the differences in the way people perceive the world, the differences between their subjective realities. PST also describes the relationship between subjective reality, or Perceptual Style, natural strengths potential, and how life experience influences the development of these potentials into usable skills.

Before we share the principles of our theory, let's pause for a moment and talk about skills, specifically, what we mean when we refer to skills. A skill is a behavior a person develops through training or experience. Behavior is the observable expression of skill.

Behavior is the application in the world of the skills that we have. If the behavior is based on natural skill, it expresses itself organically and in a manner that grows and deepens continuously and is responsive to the changing world.

If the behavior is based on acquired skill, it becomes part of a script—mimicry, blind performance. When circumstances change, the behavior is not transportable, and a new script is needed.

Our focus in behavior development is on observable or demonstrable action that is conscious and measurable and based on natural skills.

The Seven Distinguishing Principles of PST

Okay, now for the seven key principles of Perceptual Style Theory:

1. Perception is the process that allows us to assign meaning to the world around us. Perception creates our view of reality.
2. People perceive the world differently and consequently derive different meanings from the same event.
3. Perceptual differences can be grouped into six Perceptual Styles.
4. Perceptual Style is innate and does not change over time.
5. Natural skills and abilities are directly tied to Perceptual Style.
6. Early life experience directly influences the development of a preferred pattern for interacting with other people.
7. The innate Perceptual Style skills that people develop and recognize are a direct reflection of their Preferences for Interaction.

To gain a better grasp of Perceptual Style Theory, let's examine each of the seven principles in detail:

Principle #1
Perception Creates Our View of Reality

Perception is the process that allows us to assign meaning to the world around us. Perception creates our view of reality.

Perception is a complex process that our brain uses to create meaning by contextualizing the input from our five senses, our innate biases, and our life experiences.

We create meaning moment by moment with our perception process, and it all happens in the blink of an eye. Over time this process begins a consistent view of the world that is our subjective reality.

Okay, that's a lot to take in. So, let's break it down a little bit further.

What are the five senses? Sight, hearing, taste, touch, and smell. The five senses provide data about what is happening in the moment. They also contribute to memories—a photo, a song, a perfume, a food, a hug—each can remind us of a moment in the past.

Research shows that the average person gets 75 percent of their input from sight, 13 percent from hearing, and 12 percent combined from smell, taste, and touch. Of course, for people who have lost one or more of their five senses, the other senses become more acute and fill in the void.[5]

Your five senses each send signals to your brain, and your brain combines them into a contextual message. Then, your innate biases kick in to create meaning from the data that your senses received.

Innate biases are hard-wired in our brains. The type of biases we are talking about have to do with behaviors, not beliefs.

The concept of innate bias comes from philosophy and psychology, which define it as an item of knowledge that people are born with rather than something people have learned through experience.

Innate biases are our brain's way of helping us instantaneously decide what's important, what deserves our attention, what takes priority. They are shortcuts our brain uses to quickly make judgments and decisions on the information received from our senses.

Innate biases are unique to your Perceptual Style. They are in alignment with how you make meaning of the world. You literally create context from the input of your senses with your innate biases. That context provides you with a starting point for action.

Let's say three friends walk into a party together. They each look around the room for a second or two before moving off in different directions.

Travis initially notices the facts in the room—where the bar is, where the food is, how people are scattered around. He heads to the bar to get a drink.

James initially notices the feel of the room—people seem to be stationary in small groups rather than milling around. He spies a group of people he knows and heads over to join them.

Connor initially notices the action levels among the groups. Some are sedate, and some are jovial. He heads over to one of the more jovial groups where everyone seems to be talking.

Each of the friends takes action based on their perception of the room—what their senses told them and what their innate biases filtered for them as most important and the starting point for action.

Before we go on, let's take a moment to explore two other types of biases we hear a lot about in the news today: unconscious bias and cognitive biases. You aren't born with them like you are with innate biases. However, unconscious and cognitive biases can impact your judgment and choices because they impact your beliefs.

Everyone, no matter their Perceptual Style, experiences unconscious and cognitive biases in the same way. You learn unconscious biases early in life, and you don't question them because they just "are." An unconscious bias is internally logical but based on a fallacy or a misconception handed down to you by parents, environment, or culture. Simple examples are believing nighttime is scary, redheads have lots of freckles, or all dogs hate cats. Complex examples—also known as implicit bias—include racism and sexism.[6]

Once you are aware of an unconscious bias (things you learned early in life and don't question because they "are"), it's by definition no longer unconscious. You can notice when you are applying the bias, and consequently, you can work to correct the misconceptions associated with the bias at its core.

If your bias is that nighttime is always scary, it can be as easy as creating an adventure in the night to watch the stars and see how beautiful things are so that you have a positive experience that disproves the belief that nighttime is always bad.

Complex unconscious (also known as implicit) biases take more work to unravel, but the work is clear once you are aware of the bias. These types of biases often accompany stereotypes (think of racism, ageism, sexism). A place to start is to begin thinking of the people you encounter as individuals and go on from there.

Cognitive biases are systematic errors in thinking.[7] These often arise from thought-processing errors related to memory, attention, or other types of mental mistakes.[8] Examples of cognitive bias include:

- Favoring information that confirms your existing beliefs and ignoring other information (confirmation bias)
- Believing you knew the outcome of a past event before it happened, as in "I knew it all along" (hindsight bias)
- Tending to be overly influenced by the first piece of information you hear (anchoring bias)

When you learn about cognitive biases (systemic errors in thinking), you can choose to take action to mitigate them until they disappear from your normal response patterns. For example, once you are aware of confirmation bias, you can choose to periodically seek out opposing points of view as input into your decision-making processes.

An essential thing to note is unconscious and cognitive biases can be recognized and changed.[9]

Okay, now back to innate biases and how they relate to perception.

Innate biases are aligned with Perceptual Style. For example, because of your Perceptual Style, you may be predisposed (a synonym for innate bias) to be optimistic, enjoy bargaining, seek out community, observe protocols, look for problems to solve, or engage quickly. Each of these is a characteristic behavior of one of the Perceptual Styles.

Innate bias is a gift. Rather than being born with a blank slate for a brain, we each have predispositions that jump-start our understanding and allow us to take action.

Perception doesn't stop with input from your senses and filtering by your innate biases. There's one more step.

Life experience plays a critical part in the process of perception because it adds validation. Our brain takes in the information from our senses, filters it with the context of our innate biases, and then checks the perception against what we've known to be true for ourselves in the past.

If we've had similar experiences before, it may flavor our perception of the current moment. If nothing in our memory is relevant, then our brain takes note of the current perception and stores it to build on later.

Perception is fascinating, as it both grows and solidifies over time. It solidifies through repetition. It grows as you gain new life experiences and awareness. The more solidified your perception becomes, the more you will believe that the way you see the world is the only and correct way.

The more open you are to new life experiences and points of view different from your own, the more your perception will grow. It's your choice based on how much emphasis you put on the life experience validation. You can choose to be "set in your ways" or to be open to new options (or a combination of those two extremes). The more open you are to understanding perceptual views that are different from your own, the more you will be open to accepting differences between you and others in your life.

Perception defines your view of reality. It helps you make meaning of the world around you. That's pretty profound.

Principle #2
People Perceive the World Differently

People perceive the world differently and consequently derive different meanings from the same event.

It's a fact. People truly perceive the world differently, and this differing perception leads to different conclusions about what is important, how things should be done, and the "truth" of any situation.

Research implies that perception is actually a filter applied to objective reality, resulting in natural differences between people.[10]

The human tendency is to be unaware of the filter of perception and to believe that we see the world around us objectively. That's where the naïve realism we mentioned before creeps in—believing what we see is right and that people who disagree with us must be uninformed, irrational, or biased.

The truth is, what you see is real for you, but what others see is real for them. Differences in perception occur because none of us has direct access to objective reality.

We all use the filter of perception to make meaning for ourselves. This isn't a bad thing—it's a gift that prevents us from being overwhelmed by the amount of input we constantly receive.

There's a lot of unnecessary conflict and drama in the world that could be avoided by understanding and applying this simple concept. We don't all have the same filter, so we see things differently, and that's okay. This reality gives us a place to begin a conversation about the differences between us.

Please note that while you can gain an understanding of how people with different Perceptual Styles "see the world," you can never really experience the world the way they do. We will say more about this later.

Principle #3
There Are Six Perceptual Styles

Perceptual differences can be grouped into six Perceptual Styles.

Perceptual Style describes differences in the process of perception that creates meaning.

We believe perceptual meaning is impacted by fundamental behavioral drivers (essential aspects of being human). After years of observation and study, we found these to be the fundamental aspects of being human that are key to perception:

- Experience—the content of participation in an event
- Knowledge—observation, learning, and reasoning
- Community—fellowship with others as a result of sharing common attitudes, interests, purpose
- Possibility—belief about or mental picture of the future
- Accomplishment—successful achievement of an objective
- Rules—prescribed guides for conduct or action

Each of us has all six of these fundamental drivers, but their strength varies from person to person, and the order of their strength determines an individual's Perceptual Style. We have identified six distinctly different Perceptual Styles.

So why six? There's no magic in the number. We didn't pick the number six out of a hat and then work backwards to define each one. Instead, we correlated all the data we had about fundamental drivers and innate bias, and the result was six unique Perceptual Styles.

Each Perceptual Style represents a distinct grouping of fundamental behavior drivers that result in distinctive perceptual experiences and characteristic behaviors.

All six Perceptual Styles are normal and healthy ways of perceiving the world. None is better than nor more accurate in its perception than any other. They each have unique strengths and specific blind spots. They all shine in some situations and struggle in others. It's part of being human.

Principle #4
Perceptual Style Is Innate

Perceptual Style is innate and does not change over time.

You are born with your Perceptual Style. It is inherent, not inherited—big difference.

Your Perceptual Style has been a part of you since your first breath. But because early childhood is about growing and socializing, it's often difficult to see the specific markers of your Perceptual Style until you reach early adolescence.

Because Perceptual Style is not inherited, you don't necessarily have the same Perceptual Style as one of your parents. There's a 98 percent chance your parents have different Perceptual Styles from each other, and there's a 60 percent chance you have a different Perceptual Style than either of them. If you have siblings, there's a strong probability your Perceptual Styles will be different. (Sure helps explain some of those interesting and challenging family dynamics!)

As a note of interest, we don't provide assessments to children before the age of 16. Our experience shows that young people need enough life experience to relate to the vocabulary of the assessments, and they also need the ego independence to relate to their own internal experience.

Some people will claim their Perceptual Style changes over time, but our observation is that they are confusing learned behaviors demanded by others or by specific situations with personal perception. What does change over time is your awareness of your Perceptual Style, not your actual style. (We do have the studies and numbers to prove this—check out the research section on our website, specifically about the reliability and validity in

https://www.yourtalentadvantage.com/Research

Principle #5
Perceptual Style Is the Basis of Natural Skills

Natural skills and abilities are directly tied to Perceptual Style.

There is an extensive but finite set of skills and behaviors that naturally align with each Perceptual Style. Realistically, you will never master all of the potential available to you, not because you don't want to, but because there's so much to choose from and only so much time.

The alignment of skills and behaviors with Perceptual Style exists because people naturally see the things associated with their Perceptual Style. Those things are easy for them to grasp, understand, and use.

None of us has the luxury of only developing our natural skills. Everyone also develops acquired skills—those skills that are not aligned with their Perceptual Style but are necessary for their survival. These are things we learn to do because they must be done, either because our parents, teachers, or others in authority tell us we must do them; or because there's no one else in our circle of friends and family that can and someone has to step up; or they are just life skills we must have even though they are not part of our natural skill repertoire.

Early markers of natural and acquired skills are the joy and the resistance that young children express towards specific activities. Think back on your childhood—the things you loved doing and the things you tried to avoid. Many of those preferences are with you today because they are related to the natural skills potentials associated with your Perceptual Style. Conversely, many of the things you avoid reflect acquired skills associated with one of the other five Perceptual Styles.

Principle #6
Preferences for Interaction Are Developed

People develop Preferences for Interaction with others over the course of their early life experiences.

Preferences for Interaction are just that—how we prefer to interact with other people, with ourselves, and with the external world.

Preferences for Interaction fall into three distinct categories—Transactions, Operations, and Resources—and each of us has equal capacity for the skills and behaviors associated with all three.

You use behaviors and skills from each category every day:

- Transactions involve behaviors and skills that are focused on achieving agreement through the exchange of information. Bargaining, convincing, making promises, settling arguments, representing, mentoring, selling, and persuading are examples of Transactions-based skills.
- Operations involve behaviors and skills focused on doing and accomplishing—answering the questions of "what?" "how?" and "when?" Planning, organizing, building, fixing, coordinating, installing, and guiding are examples of Operations-based skills.

- Resources involve behaviors and skills focused on enabling yourself or others by providing information, action, or support. Defining strategies, researching, teaching, counseling, sharing, advising, coaching, and connecting people are examples of Resources-based skills.

As we interact—from early childhood through young adulthood—skills and behaviors that fall into each of the three Preferences for Interaction (PFI) categories get differentially reinforced or blocked.

Reinforcement and blocking come from the environment and from significant authority figures in our lives—think of parents, teachers, clergy, and extended family, for example. This process of reinforcement and blocking determines the order of your Preferences for Interaction. Each of us likes one PFI more than the other two and one less than the other two (that, of course, leaves one in the middle).

Principle #7
Recognized Skills Are a Reflection of PFI

The innate Perceptual Style skills that people recognize and develop are a direct reflection of their Preferences for Interaction.

The process of PFI development is reflected in the skills that people develop and enjoy. For example, suppose the majority of a person's developed natural skills reflect a preference for Resources. In that case, we know that interacting from a Resource perspective received more support, validation, and reinforcement than Transactions or Operations.

PFI development creates a structure within which potential natural skills are left undeveloped. These natural skill potentials do not disappear but remain available to us throughout our lifetime. They are the basis for personal growth.

The Validity of Perceptual Style Theory

There's one more aspect of a style theory that's very important. To truly be a valid theory, what it describes and attempts to explain must be measurable.

That's where our assessments come in. We have two:

- Perceptual Style Assessment (PSA), designed to measure an individual's specific Perceptual Style
- Recognized Strengths Profile (RSP), designed to measure an individual's Preferences for Interaction and "point-in-time" Perceptual Style strengths awareness

Both of our assessments are scientifically designed and well researched. Most importantly, formal research studies indicate both assessments have high reliability and validity ratings.[11] Why should you care? Because those ratings demonstrate that the assessments measure what they say they measure, and they do it consistently, every time.

Key Points

- Perceptual Style Theory is based on the hypothesis that the different ways individuals perceive the world form the basis for their natural potential, strengths, and how they interact with others.
- Perception is a complex process that our brains use to create meaning by contextualizing the input from our five senses, our innate biases, and our life experiences.
- Perceptual Style Theory is built on seven key principles:

1. Perception is the process that allows us to assign meaning to the world around us. Perception creates our view of reality.
2. People perceive the world differently and consequently derive different meanings from the same event.
3. Perceptual differences can be grouped into six Perceptual Styles.
4. Perceptual Style is innate and does not change over time.
5. Natural skills and abilities are directly tied to Perceptual Style.

6. Early life experience directly influences the development of a preferred pattern for interacting with other people.
7. The innate Perceptual Style skills that people develop and recognize are a direct reflection of their Preferences for Interaction.

- Perceptual Style is measurable, and our assessments have high reliability and validity ratings.

SECTION TWO

Perceptual Style Defines Your Reality

Caleb, Amy, and their two teenage daughters, Jennifer and Grace, all dreaded dinner. The food was good, but the conversation was tense more often than not.

The intention of dinnertime was to spend time together, talk about one another's activities during the day, laugh, and enjoy each other. The reality was different.

Amy loved to tell stories and share experiences but found herself being interrupted and challenged for details and facts all the time.

Caleb enjoyed exploring cause and effect and gathering information long after everyone else was bored.

Jennifer was worried about the tense interactions and was constantly trying to smooth ruffled feathers with her sister and parents.

Grace was trying to solve the problems she thought she heard and pushed everyone to talk about what she wanted to talk about.

Dinner was not fun.

Then Amy attended a conference about Perceptual Style. She came home and shared what she had learned and suggested they should each learn about their own Perceptual Style.

A few months later, Amy called and told us that the change in the family dinnertime experience was amazing. Conversa-

tions that would have previously resulted in one or more people stomping away from the table were now depersonalized and handled with a respect for different points of view. Amy said the family had never felt closer to one another.

Perceptual Style gave them a common language to understand their differences and appreciate each other on an entirely new level.

Meet the Six Perceptual Styles

All our knowledge has its origins in our perceptions.
—Leonardo da Vinci

Have you ever been in a disagreement with someone and felt that you and that person were living on entirely different planets and definitely not talking about the same thing? Or perhaps in the middle of sharing your memory of an experience with some friends, one friend, who was with you in the experience, interrupts to say, "No, that's not what happened. What I remember is ..."

We've all been there, attempting to prove our point and convince someone that we are "right" (and consequently, that they are "wrong") with no success. The conflict arises from our assumption that there is only one objective reality, and everyone is more or less aware of it (if they are paying attention).

Research implies that not only is this not true, but perception is actually a filter applied to objective reality, resulting in natural differences—differences that we call Perceptual Style. Each of the six Perceptual Styles describes a high-level, distinct, and consistent way of perceiving the world.

To review what we learned about Perceptual Style from the previous section Perceptual Style is the characteristic way you take in information through your five senses and make that information meaningful to you. Your Perceptual Style acts as a filter between sensation and understanding. It is at the core of who you are and impacts your values, beliefs, feelings, and psychology.

Your Perceptual Style is the foundation of all of your natural skills—the abilities you have the potential to truly excel at with grace and ease because of the way you see and experience the world around you.

Everyone has one of six unique Perceptual Styles that is innate. Our individual Perceptual Style is literally hardwired in us and has grown with us as we've aged and developed.

The decisions you make, the actions you take, and the directions you choose are all influenced by your Perceptual Style. Your Perceptual Style defines your reality.

All six Perceptual Styles provide distinctly different experiences of the world. These differences result in a profound psychological and perceptual diversity that is the most essential diversity there is. It helps explain the differences between the ways people think and take action.

Everyone has one Perceptual Style that is innate and unchanging. You were born with it. Your awareness and depth of understanding of it evolve as you grow, but your Perceptual Style doesn't change.

Research to date confirms all six Perceptual Styles are evenly distributed in the general population. There is no difference regarding gender, race, or culture.[12]

Your Perceptual Style is not just an entertaining psychological concept but a fundamental part of who you are.

Awareness of the other five Perceptual Styles and how they differ from you provides incredible insights about your relationships with family and friends.

What you see is real for you, but what others see is real for them. We all use the filter of perception to make meaning for ourselves.

To understand why someone sees things differently than we do and that they aren't intentionally trying to be stubborn or argumentative, we need to look at perceptual experience.

The Six Perceptual Styles

So, let's take a brief look at each of the six Perceptual Styles to get a feel for the six different perceptual experiences and characteristic behaviors.

Activity

People with the Activity Perceptual Style perceive the world as a dynamic and exciting experience enhanced by a personal network of family, friends, and acquaintances.

They know they can't absorb the full richness of an experience unless they are engaged and participating in it. They are very active people who always seem to be doing something.

Activity people love to tell stories and anecdotes, sometimes to make a point, but many times just to share their experience.

They have a gift for connecting quickly with others. They make friends rapidly and effortlessly, transforming impersonal contact into personal connection. In this way, they cultivate extensive networks of friends and associates. They use these networks to connect people with mutual needs.

Activity people build confidence, trust, and loyalty within their networks by their eagerness to respond, natural warmth, acceptance, and understanding.

They are engaging communicators who charm with an anecdotal and personal style that draws others in.

They find it hard to communicate bare facts and data because that type of communication strips the topic of its contextual richness. When they listen, they are on the lookout for key points and context as clues to help them understand what is being said.

Activity people bring energy and vitality to just about everything they do, and they are often instrumental in getting things started.

They inject humor into most situations as they believe life should be fun as well as productive.

They quickly develop an intense fascination with things that capture their imagination and sometimes find it hard to resist the next shiny object that comes along.

Their world is a complex one in which very little is static. The pieces are constantly reconnecting into new patterns and relationships. Direction, ideas, and pursuits emerge as the result of constant action and involvement with others and their surroundings.

Activity people are uninterested in things they find tedious or no longer hold their curiosity. They move rapidly from one experience to the next. They avoid repetitive tasks and environments that they judge to be dull, boring, or routine.

They draw on knowledge and previous experience from seemingly unrelated sources to create original and distinctive approaches and results. Why do something the same way twice when there might be a new and more interesting way to approach it?

They find more enjoyment in activities that include members of their personal network. Positive responses from their personal network are what drives them, and to that end, they actively work to cultivate and sustain that network.

Activity Highlights:

- Jump into life with both feet.
- Cultivate extensive networks of friends and associates.
- Communication approach—share experience using lots of anecdotes and examples.
- Conflict response—persuade and build alliances.
- Key values—networking, interrelating, belonging.
- Unique in the way they resource, coordinate, and include others.

Adjustments

People with the Adjustments Perceptual Style see the world as a complex interconnection of objective processes, information, and people. They are keen and thoughtful observers of the world.

They pursue the acquisition and application of knowledge as the basis for their life experience.

They enjoy sharing their knowledge with others, and they are good at explaining and describing complex, detailed, or technical information.

Adjustment people have a strong sense of diplomacy, and they project a calm certainty. They are gifted at building agreements and making everyone feel their point of view is understood and respected.

They are careful and competent communicators who effectively use nuance, refinement, and precision in language. They have a genuine appreciation for the structure of language and correct grammar.

Adjustment people are patient listeners who grasp both the literal and symbolic meanings in others' communication.

Their thoroughness, patience with repetitive tasks, and desire for perfection allow them to spot where information is missing or fuzzy. They edit the written work of others effectively.

Adjustments people actively polish and hone their knowledge, systems, and processes to increase elegance and accuracy. They are at their best when given the time to do things carefully and systematically.

Time pressure, competition, and a drive for the bottom line all violate their view of the world. They believe these conditions lead to a false sense of urgency and impulsive actions based on incomplete understanding.

They are intrigued by exploring ideas when the exploration is characterized by careful and comprehensive analysis that leads to steady evolutionary change.

Adjustments Highlights:

- Strong sense of diplomacy.
- See objective reality, including complexity and ripple effects.
- Communication approach—share information with lots of details.
- Conflict response—negotiate and research.
- Key values—compromise, efficiency, consistency.
- Unique in the way they create routine, perfect things, and negotiate agreements.

Flow

People with the Flow Perceptual Style see a richly textured world where the pieces fit together and support and depend on each other.

They trust in the continual flow of experience and believe what is important and necessary will emerge as a matter of course. They tend to avoid pushing, demanding, or abrupt action because they trust things will fall into place when the time is right.

They see complex connectivity among seemingly unrelated people, environments, and situations. Flow people intuitively see the impacts and ripple effects of change on the people involved. They know the connections they see are not always apparent to others, and so they will take the time to explain patiently.

Flow people believe in and value the underlying harmony and cooperation they see as inherent in the world. They value history and tradition and honor the continuity between past, present, and future. They believe people who do not remember the past are doomed to repeat it.

Flow people create and sustain powerful but personal relationships that create and hold communities (family, friends, co-workers, etc.) together. They build connections with other people steadily and patiently because they know relationships require time. People respond to their personal engagement and the warmth and concern they show others.

Flow people are careful communicators, ensuring they've thought about what they want to say before they say it. They often use metaphors and symbolic language to convey relationally complex and difficult subjects.

Flow people are good listeners who are attentive, receptive, and responsive to the speaker. They will respond only after they've had time to reflect on the deeper meanings implied by the content of what they've heard. They often take time to listen to others who are troubled or just want to talk.

Flow people know conflict can tear relationships and communities apart. They are skilled at diffusing it by focusing on common ground, channeling those in conflict in new directions, and soothing ruffled feathers.

They are excellent administrators who interpret policy and procedure for their community. It is important to them that outsiders accurately perceive the value of the community.

Flow Highlights:

- Create community.
- Instinctive advocates for shared values and objectives.
- Communication approach—make connections by highlighting commonalities and sharing insights.
- Conflict response—harmonize and seek consensus.
- Key values—cooperation, harmony, community.
- Unique in the way they collaborate, nurture relationships, and guide the present while honoring the past.

Goals

People with the Goals Perceptual Style see a world in which possibilities combine with facts to create objectives to achieve, problems to solve, and advantages to seize.

They approach everything they do with intense energy. They have a high level of endurance that allows them to push themselves long after others have given up.

Goals people thrive on challenges posed by immediate problems that need solving, and they believe there is one right way to solve them. They make decisions and judgments quickly.

Their interactions are direct, uncomplicated, and frank. They approach others directly and bluntly and want the same in return.

Goals people see a world full of clear, simple options, with little ambiguity and little gray. They know that the right way to proceed is the one that is the simplest and most direct.

Goals people distrust complexity, subtlety, and solutions that evolve slowly over time. They believe the world is difficult but not complex, so they dismiss shading and nuance as irrelevant. They believe that if a problem needs a solution, there is no time like the present to solve it.

Goals people stride through life focused on the accomplishment of specific results and well-defined objectives. They experience a sense of urgency and clarity of purpose and believe achievement is primary while method or process is secondary.

They evaluate all activities based on the possible contribution towards the achievement of the results they expect. What needs to be done next is obvious to them, so they do not understand why others around them do not see and act on it.

Goals people are strong and confident communicators who speak with clarity and strength of opinion. They are focused listeners who want facts and progress updates from a conversation rather than social pleasantries.

They approach life as a competition. If they find no other worthy competitor, they will compete with themselves to see how far they can push themselves in terms of speed, quantity, and endurance.

Goals people are decisive in crises and adept at bringing structure out of chaotic situations. Their single-minded focus allows them to see the fundamental issues in problem situations, determine the most important task, and prioritize the necessary steps to accomplish their goal. Their willingness to act and take responsibility when others are feeling unsure generates respect and influence.

Goals Highlights:

- Clarity of direction.
- Sense of urgency; focus on accomplishment, results.
- Communication approach—purposeful, direct, and intentional.
- Conflict response—confront and solve.

- Key values—completion, discipline, and examination of facts.
- Unique in the way they focus, problem-solve, and take quick action.

Methods

People with the Methods Perceptual Style perceive a sensible, logical, and factual world, and their approach is rational and matter-of-fact. Things are what they are.

They see a world is full of things to be done and responsibilities to master. They naturally focus on how things need to be done and will discern the best approach or technique to apply to any specific situation in order to deliver reliable, repeatable outcomes. They know even the most complex task can always be broken down into a sequence of simple steps.

Methods people believe the facts, when properly presented, will speak for themselves. They use a rational application of facts to make decisions and solve problems.

Methods people use language to describe rather than to embellish. They describe what they see, simply, logically, and clearly. They are good listeners who gather data fairly and impartially.

They take people at face value. They say what they mean, mean what they say, and expect others to do the same.

Methods people analyze, manipulate, and apply facts. They use a rational application of empirical data to make decisions and solve problems, and they are confident that through this method, they will arrive at the correct conclusion. They strive to be objective and fair, to act as an expert who understands and presents the facts and logic of a situation.

They are gifted at bargaining because they are armed with the facts and apply rationality and logic as the basis for trade-offs, concessions, and agreements.

Methods people are factual and consistent in high-pressure environments. Their ability to see structure and impose order allows them to help others function in the face of chaos and uncertainty.

Methods Highlights:

- Practical and matter-of-fact.
- Create order because properly followed steps will produce desired results.
- Communication approach—provide facts, data, structure, rules, and proven practices.
- Conflict response—explain and analyze.
- Key values—impartiality, productivity, rationality.
- Unique in the way they bargain, organize, and play by the rules.

Vision

People with the Vision Perceptual Style perceive the world as a place of infinite possibilities, full of options and opportunities.

They pursue opportunities where they can have an impact, make a difference, and leave their mark.

They approach life as a journey toward the future. They face the realities of a situation with serious intent, an optimistic perspective that a solution will be found, and confidence that there are always other alternatives to explore.

Vision people rely on their intuition and make decisions with ease based on current information. They'll change direction on a dime as new information becomes available.

They engage easily with others but listen just long enough to get a sense of what is being said and then respond decisively.

Vision people are highly persuasive and easily convince and inspire others to join them. Their excitement and commitment are contagious.

Vision people work well with incomplete and partial information and do not need all the details to set a course and engage in action.

They intuitively see new directions that others do not and make the most of this advantage by moving decisively. This ability to intuit new, useful directions and take swift advantage of opportunities as they arise gives them a strategic edge over others.

They downplay the risks associated with a chosen course of action, relying on their intuition to deal with whatever problems arise. They view failure as only a temporary setback.

Vision people change direction when progress towards achievement of their vision is slow or blocked. As they move forward, they constantly tinker, experiment, and improvise with their actions to increase the likelihood of success. They are strongly committed to achieving their vision but are incredibly flexible about the path taken to get there.

They think non-linearly about problems, use their intuition, and try multiple possible solutions as they troubleshoot to find what's not working as it should.

Vision people see multiple successful scenarios, and they coordinate complex information and activities so that all efforts lead towards success.

Vision Highlights:

- Intuitively see new directions, possibilities, and potential.
- Highly persuasive and easily convince others.
- Communication approach—inspire, influence, and motivate.
- Conflict response—engage and regroup.
- Key values—improvisation, ingenuity, and insight.

- Unique in the way they take risks, improvise, and imagine what can be.

Do you see yourself in one of the styles? At a summary level, it's sometimes hard to decide between two of them. And it's important to note that you may not relate to all aspects of your Perceptual Style, but you'll know it's yours when 80% or more of the details fit.

The best way to determine your Perceptual Style is to take the Perceptual Style Assessment (PSA). You'll find instructions for accessing the PSA in the last section of this book.

Key Points

- Your Perceptual Style defines your reality.
- There are six Perceptual Styles, and each provides a distinctly different experience of the world. These differences result in a profound psychological and perceptual diversity.
- Your Perceptual Style is the foundation of all of your natural skills.
- Perceptual Style is innate. Your individual Perceptual Style is hard-wired and has grown with you as you age and develop.
- Our research confirms all six Perceptual Styles are evenly distributed in the general population, and there is no difference regarding gender, race, or culture.
- Your Perceptual Style is not just an entertaining psychological concept but a real part of who you are.
- Awareness of the other five Perceptual Styles and how they differ from you provides incredible insights into your relationships with family and friends.

How Perceptual Styles Relate to Each Other

All things are bound together. All things connect.
—Chief Seattle

Have you ever heard someone say, "Opposites attract" and "Birds of a feather flock together"?

There's definitely some truth in both of those proverbs. But it's also true that opposites repel, and birds of a feather get bored with each other.

Perceptual Style helps to explain interpersonal dynamics like attraction and aversion.

There is a well-defined theoretical relationship between the six Perceptual Styles. If we think of perceptual reality as a big circle, then each Perceptual Style has its very own "slice of the pie":

Diagram 1
The Perceptual Style Wheel

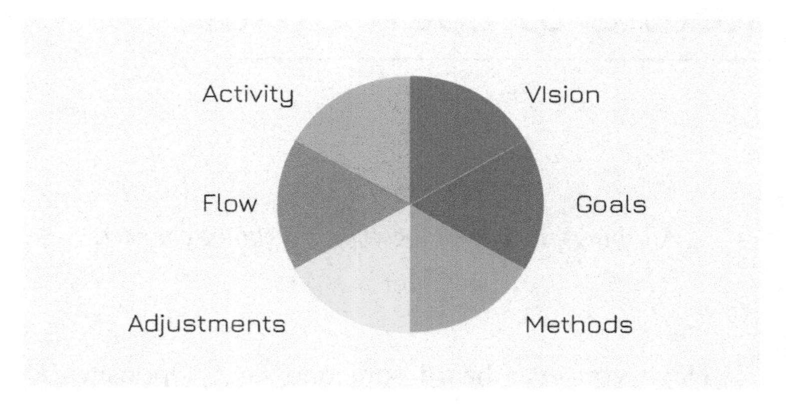

A couple of comments about the pie chart:

- There's no top or bottom to the chart, you can spin it any way you want, but the styles always remain in the same relationships.
- The colors have no meaning—other than to make the chart cute.

Each Perceptual Style has one direct Opposite, two next-door Neighbors (one on each side), and two One-Offs (neither a Neighbor nor an Opposite). Let's look at each relationship in a bit more detail.

Opposites

The opposite of every great idea is another great idea.
—Niels Bohr

Diagram 2
The Opposites Wheel

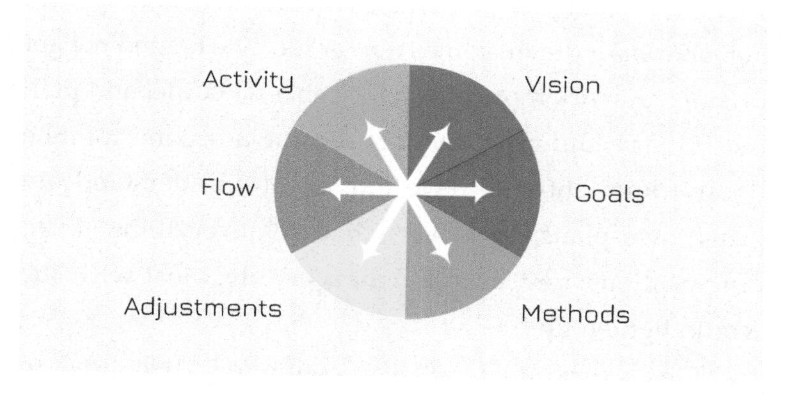

People with the Opposite Perceptual Style from yours are pretty evident from the start. The fascinating thing about Opposites is that we are all intuitively aware of what we don't do, and we admire people who can do those things. So, initially, opposites can be incredibly attractive. But with time, one of two things happen—either you develop a complementary relationship, with each of you valuing what the other person does that you don't; or you start trying to change the other person to do things your way. The very things that initially attracted you to the other become the things that push you apart. Communication with your Opposite Perceptual Style will either be very rewarding or very frustrating.

A great place to observe how Opposites both attract and repel each other is in couple's therapy. One good example from Gary's days in private practice involved an Activity man and a Methods woman. They arrived in the consulting room, barely able to talk to each other without anger and vitriol.

"She's changed," accused the man, "when I first met her, she was a dream come true for me. She helped me get organized, work more effectively on a schedule, and plan out my day. But now, she has become a taskmaster. She doesn't know how to have fun, doesn't understand my jokes, over-plans, and over-schedules everything. Even our vacations are tied to a tight schedule. I just wish she would lighten up!"

"Oh, he should talk!" she countered, "He used to bring me such joy. He helped me discover that life is not all about accomplishment and to laugh, cut up, and act silly. But now, he has turned into a clown. Everything is a joke to him. He doesn't understand that life is more than just sitting around talking all the time and having a good time. He makes light of the things I accomplish. I just wish he would be serious about life."

What initially attracted this couple to each other is now the very thing driving a wedge between them and threatening their marriage. The differences in each of their "hows" destroyed their "what."

On the other hand, Lynda-Ross has a good friend (and client), Jim, who is Adjustments, and his wife, Nancy, is

Vision. They've had lots of ups and downs over the years, as most people do—injuries, family squabbles, illness, work issues, school decisions, etc. Yet, they've raised three great kids and have a strong marriage. What's the key to their success? During dinner with them one evening, they shared their perspective. (Spoiler alert: they lean on each other's strengths.)

"I'm the planner of the family," Jim said. Two of their boys rolled their eyes and smiled. "Okay," laughed Jim, "maybe I enjoy planning more than anyone else in the family, so it's lucky for the rest of you!"

"I'm happy you do," said Nancy. "I don't enjoy it, and I don't enjoy doing all the research you do. Thanks to you, I don't have to! I'd much rather be the idea person and let you take the lead on sorting out the details."

The two sons laughed out loud. "It's so true," said one. "Mom is the 'let's try this' person, and Dad is the 'wait a second, let's think about that' person." Everyone smiled.

Jim and Nancy found a way to balance their strengths. They make big decisions together after considering what each of them has brought to the process. They are openly appreciative of what the other person does that they don't. They've learned over the years to insist on agreement regarding the "what" of their lives, but they are willing to compromise on the "how." That's an example of Opposites who make it work.

Neighbors

It's a beautiful day in the neighborhood, a beautiful day for a neighbor. Would you be mine; could you be mine?
—Fred Rogers

Diagram 3
The Neighbors Wheel

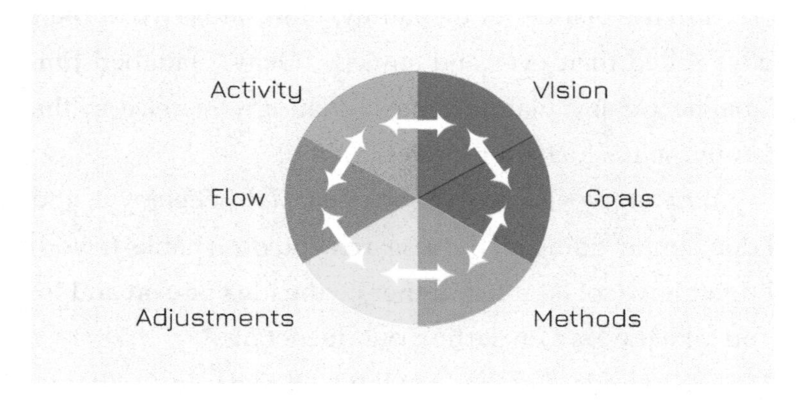

A person with a Neighbor Perceptual Style will seem to have some apparent similarities with you. At first blush, it feels like you are both on the same page, but given a little time (very little time), you turn out to have differences that catch you off guard.

The communication challenges that arise are often based on stylistic differences (how) rather than content differences (what).

If the specifics about the "what" are not discussed, you'll be surprised when you discover that the details you thought the other person agreed with you on were actually nowhere in their thinking.

If the "how" is left unspecified, you are surprised by each other's actions and often find them lacking something—inadequate, incomplete, or just off target.

Years ago, we did some training for a delinquent payments collection department of a mortgage lending company. We taught them about Perceptual Style and then helped them tap into their natural strengths to be effective collectors.

While preparing the training curriculum, we met with two supervisors, Nick and Sofia, to review current procedures and effectiveness measurements.

Nick showed us the detailed procedures he asked his team to follow. The procedures covered things like leaving messages requesting callbacks and approaching a collection telephone call with a homeowner. His procedures had options based on how many times the collector had interacted with the homeowner and how delinquent the payments were.

Sofia nodded in agreement several times while Nick was talking about the procedures. When he concluded, she said, "My team uses the same procedures, but I've taken them to the next level. I created scripts for each type of conversation, and all my folks have to do is read the script."

Nick looked surprised. He and Sofia got into a detailed discussion about whether scripts were necessary. Nick's position was that the procedures were detailed enough and covered all the possibilities that collectors needed to guide their conversations. Sofia insisted that the scripts added value because they provided a step-by-step method that guaranteed the collectors would get better results. While they were in total agreement about the need for standard procedures and clear objectives for the collectors, their conversation that day ended in a stalemate. Neither person could see the value or applicability of the details the other person championed.

Nick was Adjustments, and Sofia was Methods. They were Neighbors talking about processes and using the same terminology. Still, one was talking about the interrelationships between steps, from beginning to end, and the other was talking about concrete steps from "one to done."

So, Nick was saying, "The collectors need to do these three steps. They can do them in any order. When they get them done, they should move on to the next group of steps." And Sofia was saying, "No, each step must be done in a specific order, the same way, every time."

It was a classic situation of Neighbors agreeing on "what" but not on "how." It took time and a few more conversations to help them understand the need for flexibility in how each collector went about their collection duties (building on their natural strengths) while keeping the objectives and effectiveness measures the same for everyone.

With practice, Neighbors gain awareness of their shared commonalities and learn to use details to avoid disconnects.

Point in fact, we demonstrate this Neighbor awareness all the time. Gary is Activity, and Lynda-Ross is Vision. As business partners, the apparent style similarities we experience involve energy, taking action, making things happen, curiosity, reading social and relational dynamics, and seeing a "big picture."

But once you get past the surface, the "how" of our approaches to each of the similarities varies greatly. For example, both of us are keenly aware of social and relational dynamics. For Gary, these dynamics are a topic to be analyzed and discussed while for Lynda-Ross, they are input to creating strategies and taking action.

Another example is the way we each define and see the "big picture." Gary sees how all the individual pieces fit together and coordinate. Lynda-Ross sees an overarching theme. We often laugh that Gary's "big picture" is a 5,000-foot view while Lynda-Ross sees things at 50,000 feet.

You may find that you "lean" more towards one of your Neighbors than the other. For example, a person with the Flow Perceptual Style may find that they get along more easily with people with the Activity Perceptual Style because they identify with a common interest in people. While another person with the Flow Perceptual Style may relate more quickly to people with the Adjustments Perceptual Style because they identify with subtlety, nuance, and complexity.

One-Offs

We look up at the same stars and see such different things.
—George R.R. Martin

Diagram 4
The One-Off Wheel

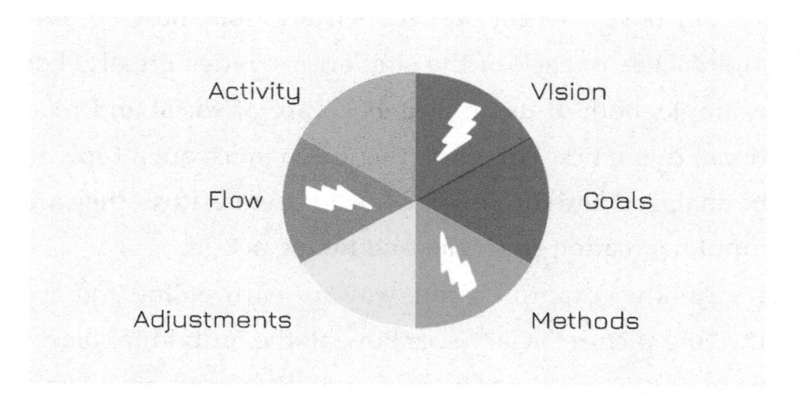

When you meet a person with a One-Off Perceptual Style, it's not unusual to wonder what planet they came from. The way that they see things can be pretty puzzling.

With One-Offs, you don't have a feeling of general understanding like you have with your Neighbors, and there's no obvious "Opposite" vibe either. So, it's often hard to pinpoint what's so different about them.

One-Offs usually feel either exotic or alien.

People who feel exotic can be attractive because they are so unusual and fascinating and don't seem at all like you. After a while, that luster wears off, and you can struggle with finding a way to create common ground.

People who feel alien are easily dismissed outright

unless there is some compelling reason for you to need to interact with them. It's hard to invest time creating a relationship with someone you find it hard to have a meaningful conversation with.

This is not to say that there are not great work, friend, family, and partner relationships among One-Offs, but they take more work than other combinations.

What does "more work" look like? This kind of relationship works well when both people are willing to compromise and can admire the strengths of the other without trying to change them.

That's not easy, and it takes commitment.

When the commitment is strong, One-Off relationships are amazing because each person shines in their own way without overshadowing the other and without trying to force the other to be something they are not and never will be.

It's not unusual to find One-Off relationships within families, especially when there are at least two siblings or when there are cousins close by that create a closely-knit extended family.

Luis, a coaching client, had a great example of One-Off disconnects. One day, we talked about a conflict with one of his co-workers that was escalating and really wearing Luis out. "Chris seems to counter or dismiss every idea I have," said Luis. "It's really getting on my nerves. I'm at the point that when I see him walk into a meeting, I immediately tense up."

"I just don't know how to get through to him," Luis continued. "You know, at times, he reminds me of my older brother Oscar. He and I never saw eye to eye as kids, and even now, as adults, I'm not sure we would be friends if we weren't brothers."

Luis went on to give an example. "Growing up, I'd be looking for facts, and Oscar would dismiss my input outright in favor of his gut feeling. I can't tell you how many times he would just skim instructions and then act surprised when something didn't work out just right. Even today, our parents call me if they need help with their smartphones and notepads. They know Oscar will guess his way through rather than pick up a manual and follow instructions.

"That's exactly the type of problem I encounter with Chris at work. He seems to jump from solution to solution rather than working through the details. There are steps to follow, and I feel like I have to redo them because he skips over them. I just don't want to have to work with him anymore."

Luis was Methods, and it's a pretty good guess that his co-worker and his brother were both Vision.

Luis did move to another position within the company shortly after that conversation. It's a great example of One-Off options—Luis walked away from one position and a co-worker to take on a new position because he didn't have a compelling reason to put effort into bridging the gap between his style and that of his co-worker. But with his brother Oscar, Luis invested the time and energy to maintain a good relationship because the family tie was a very compelling reason.

Same Style / Kindred Spirits

Friendship is born at that moment when one person says to another,
"What! You too? I thought I was the only one."
—C.S. Lewis

Diagram 5
Same Style/Kindred Spirits

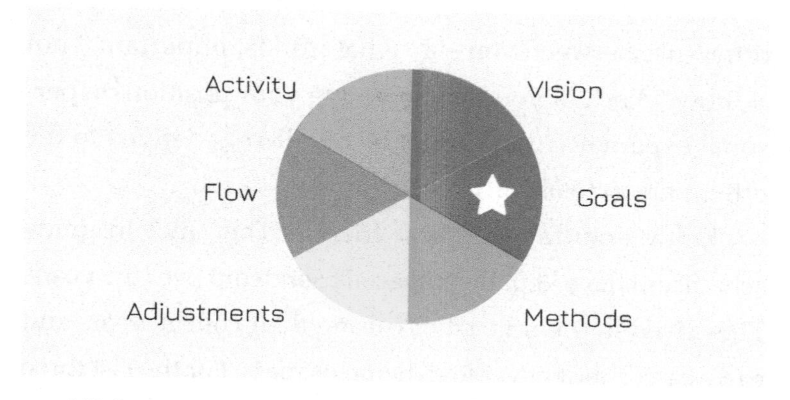

With Neighbors, Opposites, and One-Offs, there's a quick recognition that you don't see the world the same way. After that first impression, it takes a little time to get a feeling for those differences and establish a comfortable interaction pattern.

When you meet a person with the same Perceptual Style, there's an almost instantaneous feeling that "here's someone who understands me." You'll experience an almost instant bond as you relate quickly and easily and without a need to explain yourself. It is as if you've found a kindred spirit.

You'll feel that instant bond and know in your heart that here is a person who "gets it."

The communication challenges that surface eventually result from assuming the other person thinks exactly as you do all the time ... and forgetting that things like life experience make a big difference.

You may see the world the same way, but your lives have been uniquely different.

When you hit conflict, it's because there is a very real difference between you—a "what is most important," not a "how." Each of you will be basing your position on personal experience that cannot be distilled and given to the other person to absorb.

Emily and Tara are best friends. They met in grade school and have kept their special friendship over the years. They lived in separate cities during their college years and early careers but never lost their closeness. For the last three years, they've lived in the same city, and for them, the close proximity is a bonus. Emily and Tara are Flow.

Emily was Tara's maid of honor two years ago when Tara married her college sweetheart. Now Tara is taking on that role for Emily, who is planning a fall wedding next year with a wonderful person she met at work.

Emily invites Tara to attend the first meeting with the wedding planner she's hired. The wedding planner has prepared a priority list and timeline with all the planning activities that Emily and her partner will need to attend to.

"This is great!" says Emily. "So very thorough and well-thought-out. I just wonder if we shouldn't prioritize planning details around the participation of our families in the wedding and the activities leading up to it."

"I totally agree with you on the thoroughness of what's been presented," says Tara, "but I think you should be prioritizing your dress and bridesmaids and activities with your wedding party. The family stuff will fall into place."

Emily and Tara are each focused on the wedding experience. But there is a disconnect because one is focused on the experience for the bride while the other is focused on creating an experience for the guests.

Both views are valid. Their own life experiences with attending weddings in the past are influencing the different planning prioritizations.

After some discussion, neither of the friends can persuade the other to her point of view. Then Emily stops, smiles at the wedding planner, and says, "I think this is where you step in and take the lead based on your experience of what works best." Tara laughs and nods her head.

These simple disconnects between Same Style people can feel more personal than any other because they trigger our basic need to defend our values and beliefs.

The key to solving these conflicts is that each person allows themselves to acknowledge they each have different perspectives because of different experiences, and that's okay. No one needs to win; just agree to move on.

And that's exactly what Emily and Tara chose to do.

Additional Thoughts on Perceptual Style Relationships

The relationships between Perceptual Styles are fun and fascinating. There are so many insights to be gained when you understand the differences between styles and how the styles relate to each other.

It is important to remember that you have only one Perceptual Style. Despite discovering traits and characteristics that seem similar to a Neighbor, Opposite, or One-Off Perceptual Style, you are not a blend of two or more styles.

Many stylistic similarities you see in yourself compared to other Perceptual Styles are due to your development of acquired skills.

Shared values can also play a part. When you share a value with someone of another style, it can seem on the surface that you are approaching that value in the same way. But, when you look beneath the surface, you'll see that you each bring different strengths to the table that honor and respect those values.

Now that you know about Opposites, Neighbors, One-Offs, and Same Styles, here's a quick reference chart to help you compare and contrast some high-level style characteristics between Perceptual Styles:

Diagram 6
Compare/Contrast Wheel Walk

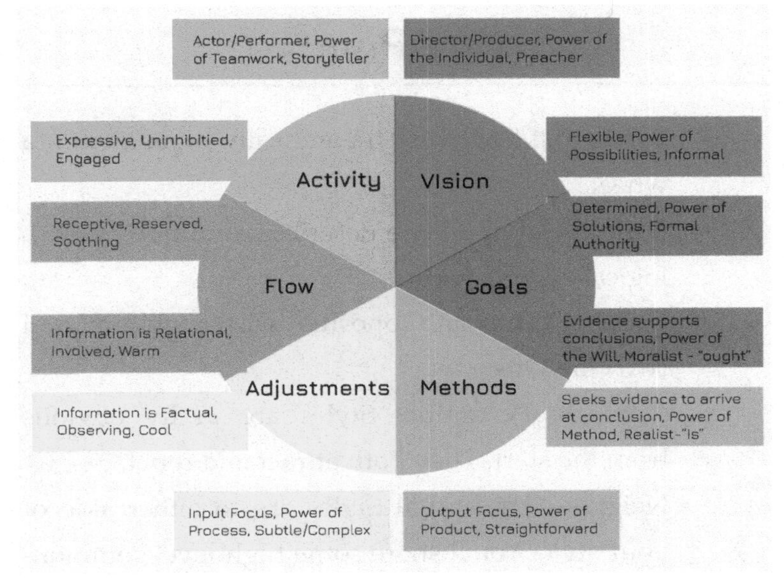

In the next section, we will explore some of the practical applications of Perceptual Style. It's an incredible tool to help you discover and build your natural strengths and also to find the best in others.

Key Points

- Perceptual Styles are theoretically organized in a wheel.
- Each Perceptual Style describes a unique psychological experience.
- Each style has an Opposite, two Neighbors, and two One-Offs.
- Opposite Perceptual Styles are pretty obvious from the start. They both attract and repel.
- Neighbor Perceptual Styles are to either side of your style. You'll share some high-level commonalities, but the differences between you will stand out when you deal with details.
- You may relate more easily to one Neighbor than the other.
- One-Off Perceptual Styles are neither your Opposite nor your Neighbor. You'll notice the differences between you immediately, but unlike Opposites and Neighbors, it's often unclear what the differences stem from.
- Same Style or Kindred Spirit refers to someone with the same Perceptual Style you have. You'll bond quickly, but life experience plays a big part in the differences between you that will happen.
- You have only one Perceptual Style. Despite dis-

covering traits and characteristics that seem similar to a Neighbor, Opposite, or One-Off Perceptual Style, you are not a blend of two or more styles.

SECTION THREE

Practical Application

In theory there is no difference between
practice and theory.
But in practice, there is.
—Benjamin Brewster

It can be great fun to learn more about yourself and your Perceptual Style. But if that's where you stop, it's just a party game. The real benefit comes when your knowledge is applied in your daily life.

Practical application takes you from theory to reality. One great example to illustrate this point is our friend Brian. When he came to his first seminar with us—a management development course—he was resistant and cynical. He had been to similar workshops before, and his experience was they always told you to change who you are and to standardize your management approach. But his boss had asked him to attend, so he did.

Here's how he described his initial experience with us:

I clearly remember two "wow" moments in my experience with Perceptual Style that happened the day our assessment results were delivered.

All of the managers who had participated were gathered in a large meeting room. Our results were given to each of us, and we were then grouped around the room by our Perceptual Styles. I remember noticing the people in my group were the folks I got along with best. That was my first "wow."

When Gary started talking about our group, his descriptions were hitting really too close to home for me to ignore. When he said, "You were the people who sat in classrooms throughout high school and thought you knew more than the teacher!" it was my second "wow" moment. I had never shared that thought with another living soul but had believed it through most of school. It was like Gary was reading my mind. Suddenly, I decided I better not discount this program. You had my attention."

Brian focused on building and using his strengths. He became very successful by specializing in what he did best. He shared that Perceptual Style validated his own strengths and put his perceived weaknesses in perspective. He leaned into what he knew he naturally did well and found a new pride in his accomplishments. His attitude towards people who were different from him mellowed. Rather than seeing differences as threatening or frustrating (as he once had), he began to see them as interesting and enjoyed finding ways to work with those differences to mutual advantage.

Our first meeting with Brian was over 25 years ago. At that time, he was a mid-level manager in a large company. He went on to establish his own firm in the same industry and achieved great success personally and financially. One of the many strengths he is known for is his ability to recruit and retain talent for his company. He credits his understanding of Perceptual Style and looking for people's strengths as his advantage.

Claim Your Strengths

Be thankful for what you have; you'll end up having more. If you concentrate on what you don't have, you will never, ever have enough.

—Oprah Winfrey

Why are we so quick to see our shortcomings and not our gifts?

The answer is negativity bias.[13]

Have you ever noticed how most people tend to register the bad stuff more than the good stuff? You've probably caught yourself doing it too. It's pretty common to remember a negative experience more vividly than a positive one. That's negativity bias in action.

This bias towards the negative isn't because we live in cynical times; it's actually something handed down to us from our very early ancestors who knew being alert for things that might harm them (i.e., negative things) was the difference between life and death. In today's world, our brains naturally give priority to negative input over positive input.

Because of negativity bias, we hear and remember criticism and correction more acutely than praise and validation. We give negative feedback more weight and significance than positive feedback, and we tend to believe negative input to be more truthful about us.

Culturally, most of our performance feedback is driven by a stance of improvement and a striving to create "well-rounded" individuals. While on the face of it, this sounds like an admirable goal, in practice, it creates feedback systems that focus on what people lack.

Think about it. The typical report card from grade school to high school rarely says, "Johnny is great at music; he should do more!" Usually, those report cards highlight areas that need improvement and suggest tutoring or extra classes. From an early age, we learn to focus more on what we don't do well in rather than celebrating and doing more of what we naturally do well in.

It doesn't stop there. In the workplace, performance reviews often put the primary focus on areas that "need improvement" and those that "meet expectations." Neither of those ratings ever makes you feel like doing more of what you are doing well.

Another thing to consider at work is the traditional performance bell curve rating system that many employers use.[14] The curve assumes that 70 percent of employees will perform at some level of "average," 10 percent will perform "below average," and only 20 percent earn performance ratings of "above average." With this system, employees who are doing well become the "expected standard," leaving little room for having their talents recognized as exceptional.

After years of practice with feedback pointing out what we should improve, we end up taking our natural talents and gifts for granted. And that enhances the inherent bias of humans to downplay those things that they do naturally well.

The things that come easily to us often don't seem like any big deal because they are aligned with our Perceptual Style. They fit how we make meaning and take action in the world. They feel natural and congruent with who we are.

You have thousands of skills and abilities that are naturally yours because of your Perceptual Style. They represent your innate potential. You aren't aware of all the natural skills and abilities you have. Sure, you might be confident about some of them because people often compliment you on them, and you listen. But you may not value others as special strengths because you dismiss them with the "everyone can do that" mindset, and still more, you just haven't developed yet because you haven't been in a situation that required them.

In any case, your natural skills and abilities are your unique gifts—the things you are destined to excel at if you choose.

The trap happens when we assume things that are easy for us must be easy for everyone. So, we discount our own talents and gifts, and instead, we focus on things we think we are missing or that we believe aren't up to par. That's the trap of negativity bias. It can create an unending cycle of dismissing our own gifts and constantly searching for what we think is missing that will make us happier.

The good news is, you can break your own cycle of negativity bias. It's a simple process with profound results. All you need is a mindset shift, awareness, and some practice.

Learning about your strengths and incorporating them into your actions is a powerful and rewarding experience. It creates a solid foundation for you to take action, understand your true value, and gain perspective about things that you think are your weaknesses or your challenges.

Recognizing your strengths can also help you discover those skills that you have acquired through necessity (you had to learn how to do it to accomplish a particular task), promotion (you were told you needed to develop the skill by someone in authority, such as a parent, teacher, or employer), or admiration (you admired someone else's ability to perform the skill and decided you want to learn how to do it too).

Skills acquired in this way are not "bad"; they just take a whole lot more conscious effort, energy, and focus to develop proficiency. You may become highly adept at these acquired skills, but they will always require more focus and energy than your natural skills. Another downside is that they distract you from developing those skills that are yours by birthright.

We've seen the impact of acquired skills over and over again in our career coaching work. People come to coaching because they are dissatisfied with their careers, but their conclusion is that they need to get better with what they do. They've pursued the skills, put in the time and lots of effort, and achieved competence, but they are still tired and unhappy.

The insidious thing about an over-emphasis on acquired skills is that it causes you to lose focus on your natural strengths.

When Lisa, a corporate attorney, contacted us she was at the end of her rope. Almost in tears, she explained how she hated her job, hated going to work, and was at a loss of what to do. She had thought she had always wanted to be a corporate attorney and now was sure she had made a mistake.

Working with us, she learned her Perceptual Style was Flow. She valued community and cooperation. The company she worked for was internally competitive, highly political, and experiencing constant change.

The issue was not her love of practicing corporate law, it was the environment that was stifling her natural skills and forcing her to function mostly on acquired skills. Consequently, she was exhausted.

Lisa identified the top 10 natural skills she needed the opportunity to perform in order to feel comfortable in her work. She created an interview checklist she could use while searching for a position with a different company.

Within one month, she had secured a new position in a company with a culture that allowed Lisa's natural strengths to shine. Four years later, she is still thriving.

Lisa's story demonstrates what happens when your natural skills are pushed aside and acquired skills dominate your daily life.

We are not suggesting that you drop your acquired skills. You acquired them for a reason, so they are meaningful to you. The key to acquired skills is to use them in moderation rather than building your life around them.

One of the goals in claiming your strengths is doing more of what you do naturally well and reducing your reliance on acquired skills, using them when you need to, or allowing others to perform those skills for you.

There will always be some acquired skills that you have to perform. Still, when you discover what they are, we encourage you to develop a version of them aligned with who you are that is built on your strengths instead of trying to mimic someone whose Perceptual Style is not the same as yours (a recipe for frustration).

A classic example of this is organizing. We all need some level of organizing in our lives—even if it's nothing more than finding things in our closets or keeping personal records, so we can pay our bills.

Most popular approaches to personal organization are written from a Methods voice. So, if you are Methods, these were meant for you exactly as they are written. But if you are any other style, you'll find parts you can relate to and parts that make no sense, and if you try to follow the approach exactly, you'll get frustrated with it and with yourself.

So, what do you do? With organizing, as with any "proven methodology," the key is to adopt the essence of the methodology and put your own spin on it. Think of the end result that's expected and adopt your own technique.

If you are striving to adopt the "a place for everything and everything in its place" objective in your closet, you have a lot of latitude. "Place" can be anything from a general area to a specific shelf or box on a shelf. You can organize by color, clothing article, or purpose (such as work or casual). The key is to organize in a manner that is meaningful and useful for you. Look to the experts for tips and ideas, then you decide on the techniques.

Keep in mind that human beings thrive best when we can rely on others. It's a fact that one person cannot do it all. And honestly, it's a waste of your special gifts to go chasing after mastering everything (your natural skills take a back seat when you focus on trying to acquire skills that others with different Perceptual Styles excel at).

It's also a trap to focus on your weaknesses. We all have blind spots and skills we don't do well or aren't interested in. No one is perfect.

Chasing perfection is like creating your own hamster wheel—you keep trying, and you feel the momentum, but the goal is unattainable because you are running in place.

We aren't suggesting that you ignore your weaknesses. But we believe that if you first understand your strengths, you will gain an invaluable perspective about what your weaknesses really are and how you can mitigate them while standing in your strengths.

The goal is to use your strengths and awareness of differences to be the best you (not the perfect you). To be comfortable with who you are and the value you bring to all that you do.

Standing in your strengths is a simple process that you can use over and over again to ground your actions in your natural strengths. It's not a one and done; it's an easy-to-use, repeatable process you can rely on every day of your life.

The Four Stages of Learning

Learning is a treasure that will follow its owner everywhere.
—Chinese Proverb

Our process for you to learn to stand in your own strengths is based on a variation of the conscious competence learning model developed by Noel Burch, an employee with Gordon Training International, in the 1970s.[15]

Initially developed in the late 1960s, the four stages of learning theory quickly gained popularity and usage in consulting, coaching, and education.

The four stages of the conscious competence learning model (also referred to as levels by some) reflect unique combinations of awareness and competence:

Diagram 7
Conscious Competence Learning Model

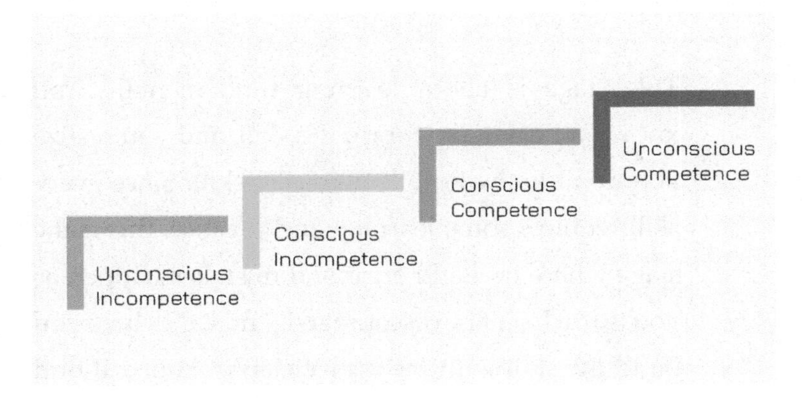

Let's look at the four stages of the learning theory as they apply to your skills:

1. Unconscious Incompetence—you don't know what you don't know.

   This is a stage of discovery. Perhaps you don't understand the skill, you don't think it's useful, or you are totally unaware that the need for it exists. In any case, you become aware of the skill at this stage, recognize it has value, realize you don't yet possess the skill, and decide you want to learn the skill. (The process is pretty much the same for natural or acquired skills.) Then you progress to the next stage.

2. Conscious Incompetence—you know what you don't know.

   This stage is about learning fundamentals. You know you want to perform the skill, and you realize you don't know how to learn the skill. Since every skill requires some learning and practice, this is the stage where trial and error and mistakes happen as you learn. Don't be discouraged—mistakes help you build the skill with more proficiency. You will find in this stage that natural skills feel easier and that acquired skills create more frustration in the learning.

3. Conscious Competence—you know what you know, but you have to think about it.

   At this stage, you now understand the skill, and you know how to do it. But when you choose to perform the skill, you need to focus and think about it while you are doing it. Others might compliment you on how well you are doing, but you know that there's a chance of a mistake without concentration.

   This stage is the stopping point for acquired skills. No matter how often or well you perform them, they will always require focus.

4. Unconscious Competence—you know, and you can do it effortlessly.

   This is the final stage for natural skills. You've practiced the skill often, and it's become a part of you. You do it so well you may not even recognize when you are doing it ... it's like "second nature." You don't need to focus on the skill; it flows naturally.

The process of claiming your natural skills and standing in your own strengths is iterative.

You create a foundation with the natural skills you are aware of, and then you continue to build on that foundation. As your natural skills become muscle memory for you, they don't stop. They continue to grow. That's the fascinating thing about natural skills in comparison to acquired skills. Natural skills grow and refine and get better and better while acquired skills reach a certain point of mastery and stop.

Natural skills take on a life of their own. They move beyond what you initially mastered them to accomplish. As you develop them, they open you to new ways to apply them, ways to refine and hone them, and ways to expand and push them to greater accomplishment.

Acquired skills, on the other hand, are situation-specific. You learn them because you have to, but it is like continually following a step-by-step instruction manual. They play out the same way every time. If the situation changes or you move to a new environment, they are not easily transferable because they were learned by rote. They have no life of their own in which to mature and expand.

With natural skills, it's like riding a bicycle—once you know how you never forget. And the more you do it, the easier it is and the farther you can go.

Acquired skills are transitory—they exemplify the saying, "Use it or lose it." It's like memorizing data to pass a test and forgetting it when you walk out of the classroom door.

Three Steps to Claiming Your Strengths

Knowing others is intelligence;
knowing yourself is true wisdom.
—Lao Tzu

Claiming your strengths is an active and iterative process. Like lifting weights, it can be awkward and painful initially, but as you strengthen the necessary muscles, it becomes easier. The more you work at it, the easier it becomes. Just like a physical plan of exercise, if you take on too much in the beginning, it will exhaust you and sabotage long-term gains.

Fundamentally, there are three steps:

Step 1 is all about discovery. It represents unconscious incompetence (discovering natural capacities you didn't know you have and that you can develop) and unconscious competence (discovering strengths you have that others value).

Step 1 is a mindset shift from the negative to the positive. Look for what you do well naturally. You will gain a new perspective when you think about what you do well rather than what you think you need to "fix."

The hardest part of this step is getting started. You'll need to let go of dismissing and devaluing your strengths. But the personal validation you'll feel is really worth the effort.

Here's an easy way to get started. Choose a few friends or family members you trust and ask each of them to share with you two or three things they think you do really well that they admire about you.

There's magic in asking for two or three things. If you ask for only one thing, people feel pressured to "get it right," which can be stressful. If you ask for more than three, like four or five, it starts to feel like work for the other person. But two or three feels easy, and people are more likely to respond with what comes to mind first, which is precisely what you want to hear.

Now consider the feedback you receive. Own the compliments; think of times you recognize yourself doing those things well.

Paul reached out to 3 close friends and was taken aback when each of them responded that he was a natural peacemaker. His consistent and constant interest in the wellbeing of other people was highly regarded among his friends and family. Paul was actually surprised, as he hadn't considered his actions as anything different than anyone would do.

Asking trusted friends and family members will definitely get you started on the path to claiming your natural strengths. The best way to fully discover all of your strengths and potential is to take the Perceptual Style Assessment (if you haven't taken it yet, check out the instructions at the end of this book to access the online PSA).

Step 2 is where you build conscious competence. You are aware of the skills you are using, and those skills get better and easier each time you apply them.

This step is about building your awareness. Pick a few of your natural strengths and begin watching for the times when you use them. Look for opportunities to use them more.

When you first start building your awareness, you'll probably catch yourself in the middle of using one of your strengths or just afterward. It's like an aha moment.

As you continue to keep your awareness open, you'll notice when you start, and then you'll begin to notice when there's an opportunity to use one of your strengths.

Miesha was naturally skilled at making comprehensive, reusable lists to guide her actions. Once she recognized this was a skill that was valuable not only to herself, but to others, she began to offer her help to create action steps to get things done. Her abilities were valued by others and that led to her being promoted to a planning position at work. That position grew to include procedure writing. All because she initially paid attention to her natural skill for creating plans.

This step is about repetitive practice. No one has ever learned a skill by just deciding to do it. Skill development takes practice. You need to capitalize on the opportunities to try out the skill and let your capacity and competence grow as you repeatedly put the skill to work.

Step 3 is where you evolve into unconscious competence. You no longer need to think before you apply your skills; they flow from you naturally and authentically.

Your natural strengths continue to grow and refine as you smoothly adapt them to each situation.

You'll know when you reach this level with your natural skills because they will be part of how you define yourself. One of our clients who has been working to improve his leadership skills recently said, "One of the great things now is when someone asks me about leadership, I'm so comfortable saying 'I'm a strategy guy. I love creating them and sharing them and helping other people build them out.' I've always enjoyed strategy, but now it just flows and that is just so much fun."

Create an Environment to Succeed

What is the one thing that stops everyone from learning a new skill? Fear of failure! We worry that we might look foolish or feel inadequate, or others might laugh at us.

Interestingly, the fear of failure takes on exaggerated importance the older you get and the more you feel good about some things you've mastered. We forget the fun and adventure of learning something new and instead remember the uncomfortable feelings of being a novice. Patterns of action become ingrained; they are comfortable and known. New actions present the possibility of failure; they are unknown, and that can be scary. Change is not always easy, even when you are developing natural capacity.

Here's the good news: developing natural skills is much easier and far less scary when you apply the Perceptual Style Theory concept of the **4Ps—Permission, Promotion, Protection**, and **Power**. We developed the 4Ps based on aspects of transactional analysis, a popular psychology theory and therapy model developed by Eric Berne.[16]

The 4Ps describe the actions you can put in place to create a safe and nurturing experience while you are learning and practicing natural skills.

Permission is the encouragement to perform a natural skill. Permission can come from the outside by people who have influence and authority in your life—parents, friends, partners, grandparents, aunts and uncles, teachers, clergy, employers, etc.

Let's say you showed an aptitude for singing as a child, and your mom noticed that you really enjoyed it. By asking you to sing a song for her or making time to sing with you, she provided Permission for you to continue.

Permission can also come from the inside when you give yourself Permission to try a new skill.

Maybe you decide you'd like to turn your enjoyment of planning into a career in event planning. So, you set aside time to research options, and you set aside time to practice. Give yourself Permission to give it a try.

Permission is the encouragement to try and the recognition to temper judgment while you are practicing.

Promotion is a demand to perform an acquired skill. We mention it here because it is an essential part of your life experience related to skill development. When you focus on your natural skills and give yourself Permission to try a new skill, you won't experience Promotion (and you don't want it anyway).

Promotion is all about requiring someone to learn a new skill that's not natural for them and imposing specific expectations and judgment on how and when the skill should be performed.

Promotion always comes from the outside, usually from well-meaning people of authority (such as parents, teachers, employers) who believe you need a particular skill, and it must be done their way.

We've met many people in our coaching who have shared that they played an instrument or played a sport for multiple years during middle school and/or high school because of parental Promotion and hated every minute of it.

The parents and teachers involved weren't wrong in wanting their child or student to succeed. And it's a wonderful learning tool to gain experience by trying different things to see what you like. However, guiding someone to have a new experience becomes Promotion when you force them to continue once they've identified they don't enjoy it.

There's a time and place for Promotion because we all have acquired skills we need to tap into periodically. But you can skip right over Promotion when you are focused on developing your own natural skills.

Protection provides shelter from catastrophic failure, the type of failure that disintegrates your self-confidence and resolve. Catastrophic failure results in a "never again" label on the skill you were trying to learn.

Failure is a necessary and important part of learning. None of us master a skill the very first time we try it. We are going to fail. The key is to make the impact of the failure small so that you can learn from it but not be crushed by it.

If you learned to ride a bike as a child and your parents first gave you a bike with training wheels and then held the seat and gently guided you while running next to you as you tried to ride without them, that was Protection. It took more than one try, but you were protected from a significant fall or running into a car or wall while you were trying.

Protection is not about preventing failure; it's about ensuring that the failures are learning opportunities that are not so hurtful that you stop trying.

When you provide Protection for yourself, it's about starting small and working up to the fullness of the skill you are working on. Mistakes are part of the learning process, so making small mistakes keeps you on track far better than really big mistakes.

On your event planning journey, you would start with small events for friends that you know well. You wouldn't start with a reception for 500 people where mistakes would ruin your reputation.

Power provides recognition and reward for a skill well done. None of us will continue to perform a skill if we don't experience a benefit. Without Power, it's a one and done.

The benefit can come in many forms. A sincere thank-you, recognition for a job well done, applause from an appreciative audience, feeling pleased with yourself.

Power makes us feel valued, worthwhile, and proud of our accomplishments. It's the reward for learning a new skill.

Celebrate Your Strengths!

Once we believe in ourselves, we can risk curiosity, wonder, spontaneous delight, or any experience that reveals the human spirit.

—e.e. cummings

Celebration is possible when you feel good about who you are and where you fit in the world. It is consciously using your natural skills and honing them into lifelong talents.

It is understanding that not everyone sees the world as you do, and that's okay. It does not invalidate what you see, and it opens up possibilities for sharing, learning, and connecting.

Celebration is feeling comfortable about the fact you can't do everything and relieved that you don't have to.

It's accepting compliments for what you do well—and acknowledging self-satisfaction in performing your natural talents.

It is letting go of the need to convince everyone to be just like you and accepting them for who they are. Because without them being different, you can't shine as brightly with your unique strengths. And neither can they.

Celebration is exploring the full range and depth of your natural potential.

You have abilities for which you have innate potential that are just waiting to be used. These skills will come easily to you because they reflect aspects of who you fundamentally are.

Sure, they may require a bit of development, but you will find that effort spent on your natural skills is productive, meaningful, and rewarding.

Exploring the unique aspects of your Perceptual Style and your natural skills will allow you to fill your life with activities and people that bring you joy and fulfillment.

It's important to remember that Perceptual Style and your natural skills don't dictate your career choice; they support how you shine best in what you choose to do. For example, if you are fascinated by medicine there are many different paths to pursue—researcher, surgeon, emergency room doctor, technician, general practitioner, nurse, the options are endless. The specific path you choose will be most satisfying when you align your natural skills with the particular job.

Key Points

- Negativity bias causes us to hear and remember criticism and correction more acutely than praise and validation. As a result, we give negative feedback more weight and significance than we do positive feedback, and we tend to believe negative input to be more truthful about us.
- Focusing on your strengths and incorporating them into your actions counteracts negativity bias and creates a solid foundation for you to understand your true value and gain perspective about things that you think are your weaknesses or your challenges.
- Acquired skills are not aligned with your Perceptual Style, and they take a whole lot more conscious effort, energy, and focus to develop proficiency. You may become very adept at acquired skills, but they will take more focus and energy than your natural skills.
- The four stages of learning a new skill are unconscious incompetence, conscious incompetence, conscious competence, and unconscious competence.
- There are three steps to standing in your own strengths—becoming aware of them, practicing

them, and incorporating them into your actions.

- When you are learning a new skill, it's important to create an environment for success by giving yourself Permission to try, Protecting yourself from catastrophic failure, and allowing yourself to feel the Power of your skill.
- The reward for focusing on your strengths is the ability to celebrate who you are. Celebration is possible when you feel good about who you are and where you fit in the world. It is consciously using your natural skills and honing them into lifelong talents.

Recognize the Strengths in Others

When we seek to discover the best in others,
we somehow bring out the best in ourselves.
—William Arthur Ward

Many studies in psychology and sociology demonstrate the reality that human beings wither in isolation and thrive in community. The saying, "No man is an island," is true. Alone we falter, together we can see and accomplish so much more.

As human beings, we are hard-wired to seek community, be connected with other human beings, and belong. Feeling connected to others improves our physical health and mental and emotional well-being.[17] So, finding the best in others is not only a nice thing to do, it's good for you!

Being part of community is extremely important in our development from infancy to adulthood. Family, friends, caregivers, teachers, clergy, co-workers—all form the many communities that help us learn language, culture, customs, and so much more.

Socialization within our communities provides us with the framework for creating our concepts of self–

awareness, who we are, how we fit in, what we have to contribute, and what we need.

What. We. Need. That's a challenging concept for many adults. Children don't hesitate to ask for help. But, in the process of learning to do things ourselves as we grow up, we often over-value or place too much emphasis on being self-reliant. The older we get, the more difficult it seems to be to ask for help. The harsh reality is that we all have limitations. No one person can do it all.

Start by Looking Inward

Find out who you are and do it on purpose.
—Dolly Parton

"Wow," said Kanesha, following her introduction to Perceptual Style Theory. "This is the first time I can ever remember feeling good about the things that make me different. I often thought there was something wrong with me. I always felt like I had nothing special to offer because I struggled to do many of the things I saw others doing easily. Now I recognize that what I thought was lacking in me was due to Perceptual Style differences. It was so easy to look at what others could do that I couldn't that I got caught up in resentment and often got discouraged. The idea that I have unique natural skills that I do easily, but others find challenging has given me new hope and a renewed sense of purpose. I don't need to compete with other people, I can just be me!"

As Kanesha's observation indicates, it's almost impossible to recognize and value other people's strengths if you don't recognize and value your own.

You're probably familiar with a mantra of the self-help industry: "You can't love others until you love yourself." Well, we are here to tell you it's more than a mantra; it's a psychological fact.

Feeling bad about yourself closes down your ability to feel good about anything. It feeds negativity bias like pouring Miracle Grow(R) on a weed.

If you don't feel good about yourself, you will feel judgmental about others because you can't allow them to feel good about themselves. Misery loves company, after all (another psychological fact).

So, before you set out to improve your ability to see the best in others, your focus needs to be inward. When you can stand in your own strengths and gain perspective on your weaknesses and limitations, you can be open to seeing what others bring without feeling competitive or inadequate.

Knowing who you are allows you to use that knowledge as a mirror to turn outwards to gain a better understanding of the people you interact with. You can spot differences without feeling challenged and use those differences to inform yourself on how to bridge gaps between you and another person.

To begin to see the best in other people, you must truly understand that your way of seeing things isn't the only way. It's the right way for you. And other people have different ways of seeing the world that are right for them.

Remember the concept of naïve realism—assuming your way of seeing things is the only way? There's another side of that coin: doing something you don't like or find very difficult because you assume no one else wants to do it either. The truth is, there's someone who really enjoys doing it and is naturally good at it, and more than likely, they exist in your circle of co-workers, friends, or family.

And that's great because it means you can let go of having to do it all yourself. Not only will that provide amazing relief, but it also frees you up to do more of what you naturally do best.

Letting go is the act of giving Permission to someone else to achieve the objective you want and need their way. Note that letting go isn't about changing the objective or your values; it's about recognizing your own limitations and inviting in the strengths of others.

When you shift your focus from worry about being incomplete to celebrating all you are, your self-worth grounds you. You will continue to grow, learn, make mistakes, solve problems, and live every day with a renewed confidence in who you are. Your ego—your consciousness of your own identity—will feel balanced.

Please keep in mind, balance isn't perfection; it's perspective. Finding balance isn't a one-and-done process; it's continuous.

Self-discovery is an ongoing process. New awareness leads to greater understanding, and greater understanding leads to new awareness. The more you recognize your natural skills, the more you see opportunities to use them and expand them.

We are all continually discovering untapped natural skills and refinements of ones we have already learned to use.

Focus On the Good You See

Try to see the good in others. When you're tempted to judge someone, make an effort to see their goodness. Your willingness to look for the best in people will subconsciously bring it forth.
—Marianne Williamson

"Several years ago," said Charlie, "I made a New Year's resolution to compliment at least three people every day. I felt like I had become too negative and wanted to improve. For the first few months, I kept a notepad on my desk, and each night before I left the office, I wrote down the names of the people I had complimented. I held myself accountable to make sure there were at least three names."

"One day, I realized I consistently had 5 or more names on my list," Charlie continued. "Eventually I quit keeping a list because I didn't need the reminder anymore. Looking for things to compliment people on had become a habit for me. In the process, I felt happier at work and the people I worked with seemed happier too. I wasn't as stressed. My whole outlook changed. It was one of the best New Year's resolutions I've ever made."

Understanding that others perceive and make meaning of the world around them differently than you opens the door to your seeing those differences in a positive new light.

Make it a point to notice at least one skill or characteristic you admire in the people you interact with every day. Make a mental list of the good things you see. Your list will be small in the beginning and will grow over time.

Two common stumbling blocks to seeing the best in others are related to negativity bias and prioritizing "how" over "what." Because of negativity bias, we often notice things we don't like before the ones we do like. Things that worry or annoy us grab our attention. But you can dispel your own negativity bias when it comes to observing other people. Consciously shift your attention to notice what you like. Assume people have positive intentions.

Everyone wants to belong and to be valued. No one wants to be disliked.

Other people mean well, and they don't intend to irritate or insult you. They just don't see the situation the same way you do. When you keep this concept in mind, it takes the sting out of disconnects. It's not personal; it's a different perspective. You can bridge the gap by using words and examples they can relate to in order to reach an understanding.

Focus on the what, not the how. It's easier to admire someone for what they do when you pay attention to the result. Differences between Perceptual Styles often manifest themselves in the ways we approach things, not what we do. The other person may not do something the way you would, but they still get good results. When you are flexible on the how, you remove personal competition from the equation and replace it with collaboration and appreciation.

Finding the best in others allows you to rely on them for their skills and relieves you from acquiring skills that they are so much better at doing.

This is the place collaboration springs from, that community is based on, how relationships are nurtured. Just understanding that others see things differently can provide the perspective to build compromise.

The hardest part about seeing the best in others is that you must look outside of yourself and understand it's not all about you. And that is as it should be.

Give Recognition and Express Gratitude

I can no other answer make but thanks,
and thanks, and ever thanks.
—William Shakespeare

"I had a GREAT day today," said Matt. "You know how I'm proud of being Flow and I don't need a lot of recognition for what I do because I enjoy listening to folks and encouraging them? But today, the team I've been working with surprised me in our morning meeting with a thank-you card and some homemade muffins. The card read, 'Thanks for being the glue that has brought us together into a team that gets things done and enjoys working together.' That meant so much to me!"

Remember how excited you were when you learned about your strengths? How great it was to feel validated? That's the gift of acknowledgment and awareness you can give to others.

Giving recognition is an integral part of connecting and living in community with others. Not only do we rely on each other for unique strengths and skills, but we also look to each other for feedback about our own value.

In the previous section on finding your own strengths, we discussed the concept of the 4Ps—Permission, Promotion, Protection, and Power. When you recognize someone for something they do well, you are helping them to experience Power.

Power makes us feel valued, worthwhile, and proud of our skills and who we are. Think of a time when someone has recognized something you do and shown appreciation. Receiving thanks and compliments reinforces our sense of value for our skills.

Recognizing others for what they do well has a ripple effect. You'll find that once someone realizes you notice and appreciate them, they will become more open to noticing what you do well. It becomes a never-ending series of ripples as your awareness of your own strengths and the strengths of others continues to grow.

Key Points

- As human beings, we are hard-wired to seek community, be connected with other human beings, and belong.
- It's almost impossible to recognize and value other people's strengths if you don't recognize and value your own.
- Before you set out to improve your ability to see the best in others, your focus needs to be inward. When you can stand in your own strengths and gain perspective on your weaknesses and limitations, you can be open to seeing what others bring without feeling competitive or inadequate.
- Make it a point to notice at least one skill or characteristic you admire in the people you interact with every day. Make a mental list of the good things you see.
- When you give recognition and express appreciation for someone's skills, you are helping them to experience Power.

Use the Power of Your Perception to Transform Your Life

"Play to your strengths."
"I haven't got any," said Harry, before he could stop himself.
"Excuse me," growled Moody, "you've got strengths if I say you've got them. Think now. What are you best at?"
—J.K. Rowling

Discovering and growing your strengths can be hard work at the start, but it's worth every effort, many times over.

Remember Scott? You met him at the beginning of this book. He was frustrated and wondering what was wrong with him because he was feeling worn-out at work and at home.

What Scott discovered when he learned about his Perceptual Style and uncovered his natural skills was that there was nothing wrong with him. Like many of us he was trying to build his career on acquired skills—because he had worked so hard to master them. Scott loved his work in technology but came to understand he had copied his management style from a person he admired, but who had a different Perceptual Style and natural skill set.

Scott began to shift his focus to his own natural management skills, using the Perceptual Style discovery process. He realized that he didn't have to leave his job or change his career path. By using his natural skills more consciously, he found new energy and enjoyment in his work. He gained perspective about the acquired skills he retained. He used them consciously and no longer procrastinated when they were needed.

The end result was that his days leveled off. The time he spent at work was productive, and he felt each day completed as it should. The overtime that had crept into his daily life fell by the wayside because he was more effective than before. He had the time to reconnect with friends and do the social activities he enjoyed. Scott reclaimed the joy in life that had eluded him.

Research in positive psychology indicates that people who consciously use their strengths in their lives develop greater levels of well-being over time. One study in 2010 concluded, "Strengths use led to less stress, and greater self-esteem, vitality and positive affect."[18]

You've taken the first step toward living in your strengths by reading this book. Now it is up to you to continue to use and grow your strengths.

Understanding your Perceptual Style and how it forms the basis for your personal strengths is an invaluable tool. The more you explore your style and delve into the specifics of your unique skills, the easier standing in your own strengths becomes.

We all can get caught up in our own egos, trying to search for and figure out happiness on our own. Part of the problem with this approach is you function in isolation, and you slip into judging the differences you see in other people as less than or more than who you are. The great gift of Perceptual Style Theory is that it helps you feel good about you. It validates your reality, highlights your strengths, helps you feel good, and opens you to see the good in others.

Driving to be the best you at the expense of others never works. Driving to be the best you in community with others is the cornerstone of happiness and success.

Understanding your strengths is just the beginning. Success and happiness at work, at home, and with friends, on your terms, is possible and much easier when you approach life from your strengths.

Do more of what you do best.

Always be a first-rate version of you, not a second-rate version of someone else.

—Judy Garland

Endnotes

1 Kevin C. Costley. *Why Do We Have Theories?, ERIC,* June 2006, https://files.eric.ed.gov/fulltext/ED491769.pdf.

2 Kendra Cherry, "Types of Psychological Theories," *Verywell Mind,* February 3, 2020, https://www.verywellmind.com/what-is-a-theory-2795970.

3 "Hippocrates and the Theory of the Four Humors," *Exploring your mind,* September 9, 2020, https://exploringyourmind.com/hippocrates-theory-four-humors/.

4 Wikipedia contributors, "Naïve realism (psychology)," *Wikipedia, The Free Encyclopedia,* last modified February 28, 2021, 21:55, https://en.wikipedia.org/w/index.php?title=Na%C3%AFve_realism_(psychology)&oldid=1009494885.

5 Wikipedia contributors, "Sense," *Wikipedia, The Free Encyclopedia,* last modified July 13, 2021, 17:30, https://en.wikipedia.org/w/index.php?title=Sense&oldid=1033435233.

6 Gleb Tsipursky, "What Is Unconscious Bias (And How You Can Defeat It)," *Psychology Today,* July 13, 2020, https://www.psychologytoday.com/us/blog/intentional-insights/202007/what-is-unconscious-bias-and-how-you-can-defeat-it.

7 Cynthia Vinney, "What Is Cognitive Bias? Definition and Examples," *ThoughtCo.,* October 31, 2018, https://www.thoughtco.com/cognitive-bias-definition-examples-4177684.

8 Kendra Cherry, "What Is Cognitive Bias?" *Verywell Mind,* July 19, 2020, https://www.verywellmind.com/what-is-a-cognitive-bias-2794963.

9 "Cognitive Biases: Predictable Thinking Errors and How to Avoid Them," *Hustle Escape,* accessed September 1, 2021, https://www.hustleescape.com/cognitive-biases/.

10 Jim Taylor, "Perception Is Not Reality," *Psychology Today* (blog), August 5, 2019, https://www.psychologytoday.com/us/blog/the-power-prime/201908/perception-is-not-reality.

11 Lynda-Ross Vega, Gary M. Jordan, and Bruce F. McFarland, "Perceptual Style Theory Assessment Inventories Research Report,"(working paper, Your Talent Advantage, Perceptual Style Research, 2009).

12 Ibid.

13 Wikipedia contributors, "Negativity bias," *Wikipedia, The Free Encyclopedia*, last modified May 6, 2021, 21:34, https://en.wikipedia.org/w/index.php?title=Negativity_bias&oldid=1021821797.

14 "Is the bell curve still relevant for performance reviews?" *Profit.co* (blog), https://www.profit.co/blog/performance-management/is-the-bell-curve-still-relevant-for-performance-reviews/.

15 "Conscious Competence Learning Model," *BusinessBalls*, accessed September 1, 2021, https://www.businessballs.com/self-awareness/conscious-competence-learning-model/.

16 Eric Berne, *Transactional analysis in psychotherapy: a systematic individual and social psychiatry* (Mansfield Centre, CT: Martino Publishing, 2015).

17 Emma Seppälä, "Connectedness & Health: The Science of Social Connection," *Stanford Center for Compassion and Altruism Research and Education*, May 8, 2014, http://ccare.stanford.edu/uncategorized/connectedness-health-the-science-of-social-connection-infographic/.

18 Alex M. Wood, P. Alex Linley, John Maltby, Todd B. Kashdan, Robert Hurling, "Using personal and psychological strengths leads to increases in well-being over time: A longitudinal study and the development of the strengths use questionnaire," *Personality and Individual Differences* 50, no. 1 (2011): 15-19, doi: 10.1016/j.paid.2010.08.004.

Acknowledgments

Over the years, there have been many people who have supported, helped, and encouraged us in the development of Perceptual Style Theory.

Among these are a special few we hold in our hearts and to whom we are forever grateful:

> Ricardo Vega, Sarah Jordan, Alicia Blake, Bruce McFarland, Steve Boice, Lynnell Brunswig, Marcia Jordan, Allison Rapp, Frank Harward, David Farr, and Jim Gabbert.

You believed in us, encouraged us, and always had our backs. We can't ever thank you enough!

About the Authors

Lynda-Ross Vega is an accomplished business executive and management consultant focused on human and technical systems. She's a change leadership expert and an authority on identifying and focusing the right talent on the right tasks at hand.

Throughout her career—in corporate settings, as an entrepreneur, and as a coach—Lynda-Ross has harnessed the power of Perceptual Style to help organizations implement large change initiatives, establish effective teams, and develop leadership talent.

Lynda-Ross is an expert at helping people successfully integrate their talents into all aspects of their lives. "The greatest enjoyment and satisfaction in life occur when your actions are grounded in your unique talents, and you appreciate the differences in those around you."

Lynda-Ross enjoys long walks accompanied by her Irish Setter Kinsey, is an avid reader, a foodie, loves to work out with the Dailey Method at her local Colleyville Studio, and is a fan of Premier League soccer. She and her husband, Ricardo, are partners in business and life.

They enjoy spending time with family, traveling, and live theater.

You can connect with Lynda-Ross at:
Website: https://www.yourtalentadvantage.com/
Linked In: linkedin.com/in/lyndarossvega
Instagram: https://www.instagram.com/lyndarossvega/
Facebook: https://www.facebook.com/yourtalentadvantage

Gary Jordan, PhD, has over 40 years of experience in clinical psychology, behavioral assessment, individual development, and coaching. He earned his doctorate in clinical psychology from the California School of Professional Psychology—Berkeley in 1980.

Always fascinated by theories about types and styles, Gary found none of the theories that he studied integrated internal experience with observable behavior. Beginning with his doctoral dissertation and continuing through his years in private practice, he worked to create a practical, usable style theory.

Gary is an expert at helping people understand themselves and using that awareness to align their actions with their natural potential.

"Building your life on the foundation of your natural skills and strengths brings more joy and far more success than any other approach," he says. "Tapping into your potential is exhilarating and rewarding."

Among his many hobbies and interests, Gary is a black belt and instructor in Shaolin Kenpo. Gary and his wife, Marcia, met when she joined one of his classes. They enjoy creating landscape, interior design, and furniture projects that they do together.

You can connect with Gary at:

Website: https://www.yourtalentadvantage.com/

Linked In: https://www.linkedin.com/in/gary-jordan-ph-d-4475b011/

Facebook: https://www.facebook.com/yourtalentadvantage

What Did You Think of

UNLOCK
THE POWER OF YOUR
PERCEPTION

Claim Your Natural Strengths

Reframe Your Weaknesses

Reshape Your Most Important Relationships

Thank you for purchasing this book. We know you could have picked any number of books to read, but you chose this book, and for that, we are incredibly grateful.

If you enjoyed this book and found some benefit in reading it, we would like to hear from you and hope you can take some time to post a review on Amazon.

Your feedback and support will help us improve our writing craft for future projects and make this book even better.

All the best,

Lynda-Ross Vega
Gary M. Jordan

Discover the Many Strengths of Your Perceptual Style!

With our free assessment, you learned what your Perceptual Style might be. Perhaps reading this book helped you solidify your style, or maybe it opened a few questions for you.

In either case, we invite you to take the full Perceptual Style Assessment and explore your strengths in detail with your "Celebrate You" assessment results action guide.

Use the code "UNLOCK" to receive a 50% discount on the price of the PSA!

Continue Your Exploration of Your Natural Strengths with Our Owner's Manual Series.

Each action guide focuses on a specific skill set for your Perceptual Style.

Made in the USA
Columbia, SC
05 January 2023